Dating Disasters and Trials of a Teacher

One woman's lifelong search for true love and her dream job!

By Mina Basra

This book is dedicated to my lovely niece, Jamie who came into our lives like a ray of sunshine and saved me at a difficult time in my life with her warm cuddles, infectious laugh and gorgeous smile. Thank you for brightening up all our lives Jamie. I adore you

xxx

Blurb

A woman faces the many challenges of the dating world and realises it's not all the fairytale she had once thought it would be growing up. She is a qualified primary school teacher and is also trying to navigate the real life struggles of what it is actually like being in a classroom, from the lack of sleep during term time due to planning and assessment deadlines through to dealing with unruly and disruptive children and difficult colleagues. This culminates in her nearly getting barred from teaching and she has to fight for justice and to save a career she has dedicated years of her life to. In her struggle, she realises that she is stronger than she ever thought she could be and that the truth is always worth fighting for!

Prologue

Worst Dates

I've had some awful dates.... But hilarious when I talk about them afterwards with friends. Growing up, my dad made it clear to my two sisters and I, that if we didn't study and go to university, he would get us married off. We were all determined not to let that happen, so we studied and went all the way, making sure we got degrees and good jobs. I became a teacher, my sister Sarita went into the medical world and my youngest sibling, Pari became an accountant. However, this did not stop my dad from still saying he would be choosing our life partners! After graduating, the revolving door of eligible men were presented to me. Every few months, a new Indian man would turn up at our door with his family. What a nightmare that was!! I was supposed to wear an Indian dress, bring his family tea and impress them. Lol. I didn't want any part of it. It was unromantic and fake as far as I was concerned. I wanted a true love story; mad, passionate, crazy can't live without you love! Anything less was a waste of time as far as I was concerned and over twenty years later, I can honestly say I still feel exactly the same way.

Dating without my family's help has only been slightly better! Lol. The worst date was when I was asked out by a colleague that I worked with. He was not a teacher, but a charity fundraiser, where I worked part time. Anyway, he'd sat next to me a few times and I could tell he liked me, but he wasn't really my type and didn't really have much to say. He'd asked me out a few times and I had always made up an excuse, but one day, I was bored and thought I'd give him a chance. As I am frequently told it's important to give people a chance. What a mistake that was!!!!LOL. We went to a poole bar and we sat down for a drink. He basically kept asking me the same questions over and over. ''So you're a teacher. What do you teach? Where do you teach? So you like teaching yeah?'' A few minutes later, the same questions. I asked him what he did. He didn't have much to say, apart from that he works as a charity fundraiser and does various drugs in his spare time. The conversation was very limited and he kept repeating the same questions over and over, seemingly having forgotten what he had just asked me a few minutes earlier. I suggested we play poole, as I was really bored. We played a couple of games, which was literally the highlight of the night. Then he asked me ''What shall we do now?''

''I think I'm gonna go home'', I replied, having actually wanted to go home much earlier, but staying longer out of politeness. The next day, was a Saturday and I bumped into him at the Charity place.

''So how's the teaching going?'' he asked me for the millionth time.

''Yeah good'' I mumbled, before quickly moving away and wanting to shoot myself!

Chapter 1 – Now

"When reality is finally better than your dreams."

I have to pinch myself that this is my life. Finally! It has been a long and challenging journey, but I don't think I would appreciate what I have now nearly as much, if I hadn't been through everything that I've been through. I have cried a million tears that could fill an ocean and felt the deepest depths of despair, which makes my reality now all the more sweeter. I am more happier now, in my mid-forties, than I have ever been before. I have a career that makes me look forward to going into work every day, my love life is blissful, I am fitter than I've ever been and I am financially sound and living a life of luxury. I feel like the luckiest woman alive… but it hasn't always been this way……

Wow! Look at him sitting there! My husband. I can't believe he's mine. The man of my dreams. He has twinkly, blue eyes. Dreamy eyes that I could fall into. He has a strong, rugby player build and I love how I feel so petite and protected in his muscular arms. He makes me feel like no other man has ever made me feel before and something deep within me stirs, every time my gaze locks with his. There are so many things I love about him. He has strength of character, charm, charisma, intelligence and integrity. When he walks in a room, he has a presence that you can't ignore. He has an air of confidence, which is sometimes mistaken for arrogance. He is a leader and can be very bossy and intimidating to some, but he is also kind, compassionate and loving. God... I love this man with every fibre of my being... and I can't believe he also loves me with the same intensity. True love........... I finally have it.

I have just returned home from the QVC studios, having spent the day endorsing various beauty products. Today I was presenting with Lulu who was talking about her new anti-aging creams. I love it when she's on, as she's so full of energy and looks way younger than her 60 years. I love my job. After years working as a primary school teacher, I finally have the job I've wanted for a very long time with a passion. I'm wearing my work clothes; a beige pencil skirt with a sheer black blouse and black heels. I saunter over to my gorgeous husband who is snuggled up on the sofa and has fallen asleep. "Hi darling" I whisper seductively into his ear as I snuggle up next to him on the sofa. He stirs awake slowly. "Oh hi beautiful. How was your day?" I look into his beautiful blue eyes and my heart surges with love and longing. I remember the first day we met and the incredible journey we have had together since then. I really am the luckiest girl alive.

I wake up and stretch and yawn. I don't want to wake up as I was having the most beautiful dream..... oh my god ...... it was a dream ... but it felt soooo real!

Wow!! I wish I could stay asleep forever if those are my dreams!! If only that was my reality...........

Chapter 2

August 2019

Its 11.30pm at night and I'm sitting on my bed. Tomorrow is my last day before I start at my new school. This is the fifth school I'll be working at in a long term capacity. I did supply teaching for several years in London which I loved, as there was no pressure and my weekends and evenings were always free to pursue my other interests; I did freelance television presenting and also charity fundraising on the side. Long term teaching in schools has not been an easy ride, in fact there has been times it's nearly broken me. People who are not in teaching will never understand how stressful it can be and how it can end up taking over your whole life with little time for anything else. I can remember vividly waking up at 6am in order to get to work at 6.30, so I could prepare everything for the day. Then a full days teaching, followed by meetings, marking books, sorting out displays, photocopying resources. I would leave work at 6pm and still have work to do at home every evening after already having worked a 12 hour day. Then working all weekend to prepare for the following week, but still knowing I haven't finished everything. Having to constantly cancel plans with family and friends as you have too much school work to do, and when you're not working, just wanting to sleep to catch up on all the sleep you missed out on during the week. During the school day, I would frequently be popping pills to deal with the headaches I'd end up getting from rowdy kids. And on top of that there would be the pressure of the dreaded formal observations. I'd spend all night preparing for them, only to have my lesson ripped to shreds the following day by the senior management who were observing. In some ways, I feel like my career is a big part of the reason I'm still single, especially as it's mainly all women in primary schools.

My new school; Riverside Primary school is supposed to be different. There is a no marking policy and the planning is all done from previous years and is just tweaked for your own classes. On Friday's the kids go home at lunchtime, which gives the staff a chance to prepare for the following week. I finally may have a chance to have a life outside of teaching. I have spent the last few years trying to change careers. My dream job would obviously be presenting, but that is not an easy field to get into full time. I even tried applying for office and receptionist jobs, even though it would be a big drop in pay. I didn't mind that if it meant I could have my life back, but my lack of experience in anything other than teaching meant I wasn't getting any interviews. My other idea was becoming a foster parent. If I was to foster 2 children, I'd make more money than I get from teaching and I feel like it would give my life meaning and purpose to help children that really need it. However, I need to have at least one spare room for that, which I don't have. Plus my parents are not too keen on the idea. Sometimes I feel so alone, like no one really understands. I've spent my whole life looking for true love.... mad, passionate, crazy, can't live without you love! I've tried dating apps, speed dating, the natural way (which doesn't happen often that you get approached by a guy you actually fancy). I also used to get introduced to guys by family when I was younger. God... the stories I have ..... all mainly dating disasters! Many of which will leave you in hysterics, but you can read all about that a bit later on. The sad truth is that not everyone finds it; reciprocated love that is. I've broken hearts and had mine broken, but everyone wants it to be two way don't they? That's true happiness. People have often asked me in the past, "why don't you just settle for someone and get married and have kids? Love might come in time." But the thing is, my heart just won't allow it. I want to be madly, passionately in love! I also want to be happy and lead a meaningful life. Sometimes I feel so alone and depressed.

Chapter 3

The Early Years

I was born on the 20th October, 1979 in Lister Hospital in Hitchen, U.K. I weighed 8 pounds. My earliest memories are going to nursery and being happy there. I remember there being 3 nursery teachers; Diane, Susan and Jan. My favourite was Diane because she was pretty with a really warm smile. She was always nice to me and would help me if I needed anything. I remember her crying one day, and feeling sorry for her and wondering why someone so pretty and nice would be sad. I remember living in flats above a row of shops, and watching my cousins play with the ladybirds. They would let them crawl over their hands and arms.

My parents are both amazing and loving people who brought me and my two sisters up well. Even though all three of us are completely different in our personalities, we all have the same basic values; to respect others and respect ourselves. My dad is a workaholic and I remember him not being around as much as I might have liked growing up, but when he was there, he was a loving and generous father. My mother was and still is one of the most beautiful women I know, inside and out. She has a short temper, but gets over it pretty quick. I remember much of my childhood changing homes and schools and maybe this was why I wasn't able to make any lifelong friendships until much later in life, when I started working. I was a cripply shy child and remember hating having to go and visit relatives or attend weddings or parties. I vividly remember one such occasion when we were going to a wedding and when we were nearly there I turned to my dad and said 'dad are there going to be people there?' and my dad looked at me lovingly and replied 'Maria darling, everywhere you go in life there will be people there'. I remember thinking 'yeah this is my biggest fear and will be my biggest challenge in life. Having to meet new people.' I now recognise that I had social phobia throughout my early years and although I am now far more confident, it has never fully left me. Alcohol helps though! Lol

Chapter 4 - Corona

November 2020

Wow what a year! I have survived the coronavirus .... So far. It all started earlier this year and has been one hell of a crazy journey. More than 50,000 people in the U.K. alone have died from the virus. Thousands more around the world. Who knows how many more will die before a vaccine has been developed. Thousands of people have lost their jobs because of the epidemic and either been furloughed or had to go on universal credit. Others have been asked to work from home. My situation hasn't been ideal either. I stupidly resigned from my job back in February at exactly the wrong time. I had a new job that was meant to start in April, which I was really excited about, but then the Corona happened and meant I've been on Universal credit ever since. After months of applying for jobs, I've finally got a job starting on 1st December. I just hope the gyms open up again.

So much has happened over the last year. I resigned from another teaching job. It was not the amazing job that I thought it would be. It was an absolute nightmare workload wise and also in the fact that I had the Teaching Assistant from hell called Shannon!! I also found a boyfriend and finally thought I had found true love. We moved in together after 6 months and after 6 months of living together have now split up. Wow what a year full of highs and lows. He was a good man, but I think his love for his kids far outweighed his love for me. We had some great times together and I will never forget those. The first six months with Steve were amazing, but then things started to go wrong soon after we moved in together. It had been my idea as I had always wanted to live with a guy. Also, my new job was supposed to start in Peterborough, so we decided to move to St. Ives which was half way between his job and mine. However, Coronavirus started as soon as we moved in together, so I wasn't working and he was. I loved the house and we got on well. He treated me like a princess, always asking me if I needed anything and he was very hands on with doing stuff around the house. We got on really well, but I think I didn't realise how often his kids would be over and they both loved doing pranks. I wasn't too much of a fan of pranks. For example, one day they were going to put flour above the door so it would go all over my boyfriend Steve when he walked in. I put the daughter off that idea and said it would be really messy, so she used a pack of cards instead. She didn't however tidy it up. Her father Steve did for some reason. I think the fact that he had split up with both his children's mothers made him feel that he needed to overcompensate them with gifts and he admitted himself he had spoilt his daughter a bit. His son's mother was already quite rich herself. In retrospect, maybe I should have been more understanding, but I just didn't like pranks and felt sometimes he spoilt his daughter with gifts, when he would complain to me about heating and water. I was contributing to the rent and felt that being warm is a necessity and not a luxury.   There were a few other issues too. Life is never simple is it. I wish maybe we had both tried harder to make it work, as the love was there and he was good fun to be with.

Chapter 5 – Teachers life

August 2021

I started work at The Rine inter-church Primary school on December 1st 2021 as a cover teacher for Years 2 and 4. I thought it would be amazing, but alas the Head of Year 4 clearly had a problem with me and made my life difficult. When the U.K. went into lockdown for the third time, all the teachers were supposed to be on shift patterns for the key worker children in order to reduce the risk of infection, but Jill decided to give me most of the days. All the other year groups had split the days equally. There are three things that make me really angry; injustice, unfairness and hypocrisy. A few other horrid things happened, so I'm glad that my maternity cover contract has now ended, but I will be paid till the end of August. I have a new job starting in Peterborough as a Year 1 class teacher, but that is only for 3 months maternity cover in the first instance.

Wow I have changed schools so many times. I wish I could find a new career. Teaching takes up so much of your life and I hardly have any interaction with men, as it's mainly all women and children in schools, which might explain why I've been single most of my life. When I do go out, I never get approached by men in bars or restaurants or clubs. I think in this country (unlike others like Italy or America, where men are much more upfront and confident) everyone uses dating apps. If I didn't use dating apps, I would never get a date. And boy have I had my fair share of bad dates! Recently, I started talking to 5 or 6 people. One was rich and owned his own gym, but he hasn't even bought me a drink, let alone dinner. 2 of the others, there was no spark. I went on 4 dates with one guy and then suddenly he ghosted me. We'd kissed but nothing else and he'd been saying he wanted us to be exclusive, but I think he had lied about his job and had no money, as he was really stingy and although he had bought me some soft drinks, he had let me pay for our first real dinner together. Two guys I had been talking to for a bit, but not met yet, and then suddenly I got this message from them; 'Hey Maria, I think I'm gonna knock the dating on the head as I'm too busy in my life right now! Hope you find someone'. Lol. I deleted both dating apps; Bumble and Tinder for the millionth time in my life!!! Sick of it and how it makes you feel like shit when it never works out!

I feel like I need a new purpose in my life and have changed my mind so many times over the past year on what I need to focus on to give my life meaning. Plus, I'm desperate to get out of teaching. Last year, I was desperate to come up with a dragons den idea which would make millions and although I racked my brain for ideas, I couldn't come up with anything original. I've also thought about fostering, but I need a spare room for that. I've thought about setting up my own Recruitment agency for teachers, but that's not as simple as I thought and I need a huge lump sum to get started. Then after watching Prison Break 3 times during lockdown and being in awe of Micheal Schofield's performance, I've thought about acting and even paid £120 to perform my own script as the defence lawyer for Lincoln Burrows. However, the feedback was that I needed to show more emotion and it sounded scripted!! Although the script itself was great. I'm someone who is really passionate about justice and that was what I was trying to convey through my script. I love peace and harmony, but there are 3 or 4 things that make me really angry; Injustice, Unfairness, Hypocrisy and Unkindness. Here is the script I wrote and emailed the producers in LA that I would be performing for my audition over zoom.

CLOSING SPEECH TO JURY (Defense for Lincoln Burrows at the Retrial: 2 mins)

Lincoln Burrows is an innocent man. Now the evidence all says otherwise, apart from that one crucial flaw which pointed to the fact that he may have been framed. Does that mean we should condemn a man to death because we can't prove his innocence at this time?

So ladies and gentleman of the jury, I ask you all today an important question; which is worse? That a guilty man goes free? or that an innocent man is condemned and killed? Think about that for a second. (give jury 5 seconds to consider)

Now all of you may have different answers .... But to me the answer is very simple .... It is far better that 100 guilty men go free, than even 1 innocent man dies or is punished for a crime that he hasn't committed!!! Why?? Well the reason I feel so passionately about that is that I believe in karma and I think in life people will always get their comeuppance one way or another. But an innocent man who is executed will NEVER get his life back!

Jeffrey Archer, the famous writer, once said that 10% of all people in prison are innocent, but even if that is exaggerated, even if it's only 1%, even if it's only 0.001%, that statistic is too high. No innocent man, NOT EVEN ONE, should die for something he hasn't done.

I want you all to remember the case of Malcolm Alexander who was exonerated after 38 years of imprisonment for a rape that DNA evidence now proves that he didn't commit. Ronnie Long ... another innocent man freed after 44 years in incarceration. Troy Davis .... Sentenced to death by lethal injection, who has now been found to be innocent AFTER his death ... and there are many others. ALL A TRAGEDY!!!

Now I'm not saying that there aren't some men and women who don't deserve the death penalty ... in fact there are some crimes that even the death penalty isn't severe enough. For example, the mother who with the help of her boyfriend battered their son Gabriel Fernandez to death with a baseball bat. For me, people like that should have a punishment far worse than merely death.

But today we are talking about the case of my client …. Lincoln Burrows. What I want to stress is that even if there is the slightest possibility or doubt that someone might be innocent, and may have been framed, then no man or woman should have to suffer for that or worse … be executed.

Again I bring you back to all the cases where a massive injustice took place ... Malcolm Alexander …Ronnie Long …. Troy Davis … (all of whose innocence only got proven AFTER they had been punished). Please don't let Lincoln Burrows name be added to that list today!

Now I'd like to end by asking you all to close your eyes for a minute. I want you to imagine that you are in the waiting room, watching a man about to be executed by electrocution. You're about to see him have 50,000 volts of electricity course through his body. Now I want you to imagine that person is your brother or father and you know they are innocent……

And I will leave you with that final thought!!!"

Not bad hey! Even if I do say so myself. But nothing is easy in life and they didn't seem too impressed with my delivery of it. So what is my new plan? I want to buy a house rather than rent and buy a car rather than lease one. I think I'm finally ready to do that again, although I've resisted for years, as I like the freedom of being able to change location and change job.

I feel strange. I'll be 42 years old in 3 months time and I don't have anything to show for it. I don't have true love. I don't have children. I've never been married. I don't have my own house. I don't even have a job I love. So what do I have .... ? I have my freedom to do what I want (apart from when family make me attend weddings or see people I don't want to). I have my health (although I can't seem to shift the extra weight I put on during lockdown). Also, I keep eating more now that all the dates are going wrong! I'm finally saving money again after years of living out of my overdraft, whilst supply teaching in London. I have good family and friends. I have happy days and am at peace when I am alone. I've spent so much of my life alone, that I actually love it now.

I googled whether there are 70 year old women and men who never found love and some that have never had orgasms and there are. The stark reality is that there are some people who go through their whole lives and never find the right companion to spend their lives with. That could be me and I am finally okay with that. Well... some days are easier than others! Lol

Chapter 6 – False Rumours

April 1994

I am walking around my school at playtime …. Alone. I'm cringing inside. I hope no one sees me, but inside I know everyone can see I've got no friends to walk around with. I feel so alone.

It's an unfortunate set of circumstances that led to me becoming a loner at school. First of all, maybe the fact that we've moved house and school so many times, but also I was now in High school and I had ended up being put in a completely different form class to the friends I hung out with at middle school, so I think we just naturally drifted apart. Neena and Alia. The first two days we hung out at playtime and lunchtime, but then because we were in different form groups, it was a chore looking for them and I couldn't always find them. I should have asked to move class but I didn't.

I drag my feet to school. It's a 15 minute walk to Hastingsbury Upper School. It's a cold, wet day and I'm running late, so am walking as fast as I can. Luckily I make it just as the second bell rings to go into class. I sit down at my desk for register and then head off for my first class. The day runs smoothly like any other day until it comes to my English lesson in the afternoon. We all sit down at our tables. The teacher passes round the English books and textbooks. As we all open our text books, Lucy

Richardson says to Hannah Thompson "Why do you keep touching my leg?"

Hannah is like "I'm not touching your leg am I? Sorry accident." Suddenly, Martha Davies pipes up "Uh you lesbian!"

"I'm not a lesbian" whines Hannah, clearly embarrassed by the insinuation. "Maria is a lesbian".

The next thing I know, it's gone round the whole class that I'm a lesbian, even though I had nothing to do with the whole incident. I can't believe it and because I have no real friends to hang out with, no one defends me. As rumours have a way of spreading, before I know it, it has gone round the whole year group by the end of the week, and worse the whole school, by the end of the month. As no one confronts me directly, I never have the opportunity to defend myself and deny it. It becomes like a bad smell that is in the air, every time I walk into school over the next 6 years. God only knows why I didn't ask my parents if I could move school. If I had, I would have saved myself six years of unbearable mental anxiety. I think this is what led me to start skiving off school. I would just walk around the streets, not too close to the school, but not too far away either. Sometimes, I would go home and watch television as I had a key. As both my parents worked during the day, I was able to do this, but I had to be careful as my mum would sometimes pop home for lunch. On those days, I would time it carefully so that I would either leave before lunchtime or I would go upstairs and hide in the wardrobe in my bedroom. A few times, I got caught as my mum must have heard me shuffling or moving and she found me. I think she was really shocked the first few times she caught me. After that, I found a much better hiding place. At the back of the bedroom, I shared with my sister, we had a hamper that we would keep toys and blankets in. I would take the blankets out, get in and cover myself with the blankets and then close the hamper. She never found me in that hiding place, even if she heard a noise and I could hear her opening the wardrobe and looking for me. I didn't do it too often, but I started doing it every few weeks, when the mental anxiety of going into school and knowing everyone thought I was a lesbian got too much.

Chapter 7 – First Heartbreak

August 2001

Where do I start? How do I even begin to describe the pain and agony of unrequited love. Since a young age, finding true love has been the single most important thing I have ever wanted...

The first time I met Sanjeev my heart skipped a beat....

It was a cool evening towards the end of August. I was sitting at home in my bedroom twiddling my thumbs and feeling sorry for myself after having had an argument with mum. I was in a strange mood.

"Come on, we're going out in Milton Keynes for drinks" called my sister Sarita.

"Are you coming or not?" said my other sister Pari. "It'll cheer you up".

"No", I replied defiantly. I just wasn't in the mood to go anywhere. As they bustled around the house, grabbing their purses and making their way out of the door and into the car, my sister sent me one last text from the car. "Coming or not?"

I had a sudden change of heart at the last minute and decided anything was better than sitting at home feeling depressed, so I text back "ok I'm coming". I then quickly grabbed my bag and coat and ran out of the door to the car and got in. Little did I know at the time, that this one decision was to change my life forever and form the foundation for all my future relationships. As we drove off to Milton Keynes, I sat quietly in the back with my sisters and cousins grateful for their company. My mind drifted off as I looked out of the window, listening to the chatter around me. Half an hour later, we were parked up outside 'Moon under Water' bar. My sister introduced us to her friends, Amit and Sanjeev and we all sat down to talk. I was sitting opposite Sanjeev. Being quite shy, I didn't know what to say, so just played with my hands nervously. Then Sanjeev spoke over the music ''Hi I'm Sanjeev. What's your name?''

''I'm Maria'', I replied.

''That's a nice name. So are you the youngest or the oldest?''

''I'm the oldest''.

''Really?'' Then he brought his head close to my ear and whispered seductively ''Well you're the prettiest of the three''.

''Oh thank you'', I replied shyly, flattered by the huge compliment. I'd never had a guy flirt so openly with me before and charm me with compliments. We chatted a bit more, before Amit was saying about playing some good music in the bar. Suddenly Sanjeev got up and shouted ''chak de fathe'', which is just a fun, Hindi music line. God this guy was gorgeous, fun, tall, muscly and a real charmer. I liked him already ... and wasn't used to guys hitting on me... and so it began.

As we walked out of the bar, Sanjeev and my cousin Amrita went off to talk about something. I couldn't help feeling a few pangs of jealousy. That night I couldn't get thoughts of Sanjeev out of my head and this continued every night for the next few weeks, until finally I asked my sister if I could have his number.

''No he's a player'' replied my sister.

She was right. I should have listened. But the heart wants what the heart wants. I insisted and my sister finally relented.

''Hey it's Maria. We met in Moon Under Water. My sister gave me your number.''

''Oh hi. How are you?'' replied Sanjeev. We then started texting each other on a regular basis. A few months later, we had been on several dates, although obviously it had never gone beyond a kiss. I was 22 years old and a virgin. I was waiting for love and marriage. It wasn't a religious thing, but more of a romantic ideal. I thought it was an amazing thing to give the man I loved my virginity.

''Do you mind waiting?'' I said to Sanjeev one day.

"No. I respect you for it", he replied. My heart leapt with happiness and joy at those words, but it was short lived, as a few days later Sanjeev dropped a bombshell. "I'm moving to Los Angeles in a month. I wish I had met you sooner".

"Oh" was all I could say, too shocked by the news.

"If I don't meet someone there, I'll come back and marry you."

Even though I should have been appalled at the idea of being second choice, I was happy he considered me for marriage.

"So you want to marry me? Why?" I asked.

"I think I'd have a happy life with you", he responded. "It's just a shame I didn't meet you a couple of years ago, before we planned the move".

"I wish you could stay" I urged.

"Well you could get your dad to call my parents and say about marriage?" suggested Sanjeev.

"Why can't your parents call my parents? The boys parents should call the girl's parents" I countered back.

"No my parents won't, as we've already sold the house and made all the preparations to move. You're parents need to call mine and encourage them to stay and let us get married."

''Ok I'll ask my dad'' I said excitedly, but also nervously.

''Oh god!!!'' I thought to myself. How am I going to ask my dad?

Chapter 8 – Life

August 2021

Been feeling sad today. I went to see my cousin Amrita's new flat this evening and that cheered me up as I love her company. She cooked me a nice Thai meal and my aunt and uncle came too. I need to buy my own flat too as I hate living with flatmates. I need my own space desperately.

I'm not 100 percent sure why I'm feeling sad. Think it's a mixture of things. I miss Mark and I'm not sure why. He hasn't spent a penny on me nor me on him. He's not the most entertaining person and I'm not in love … yet. But I liked him. I liked being with him. I liked his little flat. I liked knowing that I had someone that only lived a 15 minute drive away and I could go and see him any time when I feel alone or things in life get too much. I liked just having him there. I miss him. I hope we meet again soon and I don't mess it up again.

Even though Mark is just as dominant and confident as Sanjeev was, there is a huge difference between them. Sanjeev was a charmer. Mark hardly speaks. Sanjeev fed me false hopes, promises and dreams. Mark has never tried to woo me or win me over. Sanjeev shattered my heart into a million pieces. Mark has never pretended our situation is anything other than what it is.

Chapter 9 – Guided Marriage?

August 1998

I'm 18 years old and have just finished my A levels. I'm starting university in a couple of months. My parents said they want me to start being introduced to boys for marriage. Since a young age, it was understood by my sisters and I that my parents would choose our partner. I think my dad thought he knew best and would be able to find a suitable boy from a good family. He once warned us ''if you don't do well in your studies or go to university, then we will get you married off''. That was all I needed to hear, to make sure that I studied hard and went to University. Plus I hated the idea of having someone chosen for me. Where was the romance and fun in that? I wanted mad, passionate crazy love, not someone my parents thought was a suitable boy for me.

''Maria we have a possible match for you and the boy and his family are coming next weekend to see you, so we need to find you a nice Indian suit to wear for the occasion'' announced my mum on one cool August afternoon.

''Why do I have to wear an indian suit?'' I replied angrily. ''I never wear Indian suits normally. I'm not gonna be fake just to impress some boy''.

''What do you mean? You're an Indian girl and there's nothing wrong with wearing an Indian suit and looking nice'', argued my mum.

''It's stupid'' I argued back and then ran off to my room.

The following weekend, it was time to meet the boy and his family. I had the Indian suit on as my parents wanted and was expected to take the Indian tea in to them. I hated this. When the family arrived, I did what was expected and behaved like a polite and dutiful daughter. After about twenty minutes, my mum said that the boy and I could have a chat and get to know each other in the kitchen. I was feeling nervous because I was shy about meeting new people. We sat on the bar stools in the kitchen. What followed was the most awkward conversation between 2 people ever. There was no chemistry, no spark, no anything! I felt really uncomfortable for the duration of the chat and I didn't feel any warmth or interest from his side either. I was relieved when it was finally over.

''So, did you like him?'' my parents asked when the boy and his family finally left.

''No he wasn't my type,'' I said gruffly.

''Really? We all thought he was really handsome and friendly and his family are really nice.''

''I didn't like him'' I insisted.

"Oh okay" my parents didn't seem happy with me, but I didn't care and ran up to my bedroom.

A couple of weeks later, my mum said that the boys family called and that the boy said No to me too. Thank god for that I thought to myself privately. This whole idea was not for me. This was not how I wanted to meet the love of my life. I must have had at least 8 or 9 more of these introductions over the following years.

A year later, I remember being introduced to a guy who was far worse than the first in every way. He was not my type looks wise, very chubby and short, but more than that he was really boring to talk to. We had gone for a walk round the village and at the end of the walk, which lasted about 30 minutes, (but felt like a decade) he was like, "so our parents will want an answer to whether we like each other and want to get married. What are we gonna tell them? My answer is obviously yes".

"umm ... I don't think we know each other well enough to give an answer to that", I said diplomatically. I didn't want to be mean, but I wasn't feeling him at all and couldn't wait for the date to end. When they had finally left, after what felt like an eternity, my parents excitedly asked me the question, "so did you like him?"

"No, he wasn't my type at all and he was really boring," I replied. "Well you need to give people a chance. You've only met him once, so he might grow on you, the more you get to know him," argued my mum.

"No, I'm just not feeling it," I argued back, frustrated now.

"But you're not even giving him a chance", insisted my mum. The rest of the family weren't any easier on me and kept harping on about it and my dad looked almost angry that I was saying No again.

I was getting annoyed now. Why did my family want me to marry someone I didn't like or fancy? Why did they keep trying to persuade me to go on dates with someone I didn't want to ever see again?

I then knew that the only way to get them to shut up was to be brutal. If I wasn't, they would keep trying to convince me, so I shouted out "He's really ugly! Why do you want me to marry someone I find repulsive?" In my head, if I said he was ugly, then how could they argue with that? Surely, they would stop trying to convince me, if I said I found him repulsive? And it worked! It was the only thing that worked! But it gave me the reputation in the family that I was superficial and only interested in looks. But if I hadn't said it, they never would have left me alone and would have kept trying to persuade me.

It's funny how hypocritical people can be. No one marries someone they are not attracted to in some way. NOONE! As you have to be intimate with the person you marry. Who would want to be intimate with someone they don't like and fancy? Unless you're really easy! I can't and I never have. The thought of having to be intimate with someone I feel nothing for, makes me feel physically ill and yet here were my family trying to convince me to do just that. I had a few other similar experiences over the next few years, until my family finally gave up on me. I remember my dad exploding one day at me "what's wrong with that guy? He's got two eyes, two arms, two legs. Why do you think so highly of yourself?"

"If he's so great, why don't you marry him? I don't want to, as then I have to let him touch me. Why do I have to let someone I don't like touch me?" I screamed.

My mum and sister looked at me and shook their heads. "Have you got no shame saying something like that to your dad!" said my mum angrily.

I didn't feel like I had said anything wrong. Why should any human being have to say yes to spending a lifetime with someone they have zero desire for? It just didn't make any sense to me. I wasn't saying anything unreasonable. It was my body, my soul, my heart and my mind. And I refuse to allow someone to enter my body, without first entering my heart and my soul. I may not have found someone myself either and it may not have worked out, but at least they are MY mistakes and not my families mistakes. Why would they want the blame for ruining my life! The person you marry affects every area of your life... and has the potential to make you as miserable as sin or unbelievably happy.

Chapter 10 – Heartbreak continued

November 2001

I tentatively approached my dad. I wasn't sure how I was going to say it or how he would react.

"Um dad I want to talk to you about something".

"Okay".

"Umm…. I've met someone and he wants to marry me. His name is Sanjeev". There was a long silence as my dad digested the information, clearly too shocked to respond. "He lives in Milton Keynes, but him and his family are moving to America in a month. He said that if you can call his dad and tell him that me and Sanjeev want to get married, then they won't make the move to the States."

"His dad needs to call me and ask", replied my dad.

"Sanjeev said that his dad won't do that because they've already started making the arrangements to move, but if you can call Sanjeev's dad, it might work", I urged.

"No I'm not calling his dad, if Sanjeev wants to marry you, his parents are going to have to call me, I'm not calling them", insisted my dad.

"But dad…. " I whined.

"That's the end of the conversation", declared my dad as he charged out of the room.

I called Sanjeev from my bedroom and told him what happened. I asked him again if there was any chance his parents could call mine, but he insisted there wasn't. I felt defeated. Then he said "If I don't meet anyone in LA, I'll come back and marry you".

Looking back, I now know that those are not the words of a man in love. Sanjeev was a player. His parents knew that too and wanted him to settle down and they wanted a fresh start in America.

Three months later, on a cold wet day in February, my sister Sarita dropped a bombshell. I can't remember how it came up, but I remember being shellshocked. "Sanjeev got married" she said.

"No you're lying", I responded, in a panicked state.

"No he got married", she repeated.

I got my coat, put on my trainers and ran out in the rain. I ran to the nearby church and sobbed. I wept and my tears mixed in with the rainwater down my face. "Why god, why has he done this to me?" I asked God. It was the worst day of my life up until that point. I cried until there were no more tears left in me. A couple of hours later, I walked back home.

"Where have you been?" asked my mum and sister simultaneously.

''I just went for a walk'' I replied, and then went up to my bedroom.

Over the next few months, I had stopped eating full meals and had dropped from a size 12 to a size 8. My clothes hung off me and I had lost my curves. I was a shadow of my former self and had sunk into a deep depression. I was doing my PGCE at Homerton College in Cambridge and tried to throw myself into it as much as I could.

One Spring day in May, I was looking through my emails and was shocked to see an email from Sanjeev. It was three months since my sister had told me he had got married. This is the jist of what the email said;

''Maria how are you? I miss you. My parents made me get married for the green card, so I could get a job here. I think about you all the time. I hope you are keeping well. The weather is always hot here which is one good thing and the people are all really friendly. Sanjeev''.

I couldn't believe it. Why did he allow his parents to force him to get married if it was not what he wanted? What was he trying to tell me? Was he unhappy? My mind was racing and my heart was beating really fast. After months of depression, I felt like I had suddenly come alive again with his email. There was hope ...

Chapter 11 – Early teaching career

August 2004

I started my first year of teaching at Scotts Lower School in Bedford. I started as a Reception Class Teacher for the first year and then Year 3 in the second. I remember being cripply shy and not contributing anything during staff meetings for fear of saying something stupid. I had social phobia for most of my childhood, teens and early twenties. I remember one teacher there who was very outspoken and rude during staff meetings. She would often belittle the head teacher and I remember cringing inside during some of their interactions. I would wonder why he took it and didn't stand up for himself. It was a weird dynamic. I would often eat in my classroom, but sometimes the other staff would tell me to come and eat in the staff room. Every now and then I would go in there to eat, even though I felt really shy and uncomfortable and would often just eat in silence. All the teachers there were a lot older than me. I remember loving teaching Reception the most as they learn through play and I would usually be working with 1 or 2 children at a time or small groups, while the rest played, so the behaviour management was pretty minimal. Plus I had a lovely class. If the headteacher had let me remain in Reception again the following year to consolidate, I think it would have been a lot easier and I may not have left the school. But moving to Year 3 was a massive change in the curriculum. Plus I had a really chatty class, so had to suddenly get used to dealing with disruptive children. I remember one incident clearly where a parent made me cry. She was a governor in the school and was a parent of one of the children in my class called Esme. Her and her husband called for a meeting with me after school one day. The key stage lead, Gary Simmons also was there to support me in the meeting.

'I don't know how a teacher can make a child cry.' started Esme's mum.

'I have a job to do and if a child is being disruptive and talking over me while I'm trying to teach, then there have to be consequences. As it was Esme's third warning, the next step is for her to have time out in another class, which is what I did. Obviously, she didn't like this consequence, so she started to cry', I explained.

'But nevertheless, I still don't understand how you can make a child cry just for talking. Esme is a chatty girl, but she's not a bad kid', continued the mum.

'If I make the exception for one child, then it wouldn't be fair to the rest of the class. I treat all the children exactly the same and they all know what the class rules and consequences are', I explained again, but the mum was having none of it. Esme's father remained quiet and let us battle it out.

'Well I understand that there are rules, but what kind of a teacher makes a child cry. It's disgusting that you think that is okay', she continued berating me.

Suddenly, I couldn't take it any more, as I was already tied up in knots from the fear of this meeting. I burst out crying in front of the parents and my year lead, as I was finding it difficult to keep having to defend my decisions as a teacher. 'Well I must obviously be a really bad teacher then. Maybe I should just leave the profession', I sobbed. It all went quiet for 30 seconds while I continued to cry. Suddenly the year lead, Gary piped up.

'Right I think if we leave the meeting there, it might be best for the time being', he said diplomatically.

The parents got up to leave. 'Sorry I didn't mean to upset you', said Esme's mum as they all walked away.

The next day, I got a bunch of flowers with a nice message from Esme's mum. I noticed that Esme's behaviour improved considerably in class after this and I made sure never to send her out of class again. Being a teacher was not easy at all, as it was impossible to do your job and keep everyone happy.

It became a bit easier when 2 young, new teachers started the following September, but I still felt uneasy. I ended up quitting my job after nearly two years there as just didn't feel happy there. The crazy thing was that I had just bought a 4 bedroom house in

Sharnbrook with the help of my dad and it was a really stupid time to quit.

I had been going out with Daniel during this time and had been with him for nearly two years. I knew he was in love with me and I thought I was in love with him too at the beginning. We had met at the gym. Every time I had swam a length, he would start talking to me and I was so shy, I would barely reply. But he was persistent. He asked for my number and said we could meet in the gym Reception to swap numbers. When I got to the reception, his friend was sitting there, but Daniel wasn't there. I panicked and left. I found out later that he was gutted. A few weeks later, I finally plucked up the courage and wrote down my name and number and gave it to his friend Chris to give to Daniel. He started texting me the next day.

"So are you a bad boy?" I messaged him.

"Definition of bad: dreadful, terrible, awful ☹" he replied. "I hope not".

"Haha. You're okay I guess", I replied cheekily.

We started texting every day and it was exciting. For our first date, he suggested we go to the cinema. He couldn't drive, so I drove us. When we got there, I offered to pay for the tickets, fully expecting him to insist on paying for the date as he had asked me, plus I had driven us there. Instead he said "Okay I'll pay for the popcorn then." I was a little surprised but didn't think too much of it, as I liked and fancied him. I thought maybe it was a one off. At the end of the date he gave me a peck on the cheek when I dropped him home. He was good to me and would tell me he loved me every day. There were only two big flaws. He didn't have a very good job and would often let me pay for everything. Also, I quickly and correctly suspected that he was dealing drugs on the side and often smelt weed on him. One day, we went into Tesco's. He picked up loads of items as did I and then when it came time to paying at the checkout, he was like ''I have no money''. I couldn't believe it and felt like I was forced to pay. Another time, we were going to order Chinese food and I was like ''shall we split it?''. He replied ''I thought you could pay''. I knew then that I needed to say something or this would continue forever.

''I feel like you think that because I am a teacher that I've got loads of money''.

''Oh from now on I'll never ask you to pay for anything again'', he said grumpily.

''I'm not saying that. All I'm saying was that I expect it to be at least 50 – 50'', I said reasonably. In fact, I felt I was being more than reasonable. We went out for just under two years. I ended it as I knew I was no longer in love with him. Plus, I knew what life with him would look like and being with someone who was dealing drugs and never had any money was not exactly appealing, no matter how much he said he loved me.

Chapter 12 – Turmoil

August 2021

Mark is talking to me again … a little bit. He's replying to some of my texts. It might not be over. He's 42 so one year older than me and he has a 15 year old son. He lost his mum to cancer four years ago and he revealed how he finds it hard to sleep at night because of it and has to take sleeping tablets. He's a scorpio. I seem to have a love/ hate relationship with scorpio's. They're difficult to figure out and very secretive and quiet when you first meet them. They never give anything away about their true feelings. On our first date, he barely spoke. I was the one having to initiate all the conversation and keep it going. I couldn't work out whether he liked me or not and this was not normal for me. Nearly every date I had ever been on, I knew immediately whether the guy was interested or not and 99.999 percent of the time, guys would always tell me that I looked a lot better than my pictures. If a guy started trying to kiss me at the end of a first date and I didn't fancy him in that way, I hated it. Mark didn't try. He was very gentlemanly like that. At the end of the date, he kissed me on the cheek. He said he would text me when he got home. Half an hour later, I got a message from him ''Hey Maria. I'm home now. I definitely want to see you again.''

Wow he did like me. I replied back after half an hour, so as not to appear too keen. ''Hey. Yeah sure a second date sounds good.''

He sent back a smiling blush face emoji. I felt happy. It felt good to be wanted and although he was quiet, he had a confident sex appeal. There was definitely something about him. Still waters have depth as they say.

Not sure how it all went wrong... well I do...

They say that on your death bed, you always regret the things you didn't do... not the things you did. If I died tomorrow, I can say I tried...   I always followed my heart ...

Chapter 13 – Moving to Canada

August 2007

''I don't want to move to Canada. I want to move to London,'' I said to my dad.

''If you don't come to Canada with us, then I am disowning you'' stated my dad, firmly. ''I have enough money that you will never have to work again and we can go travelling around the world together''. Hmmm that did sound fun … but would it be fun doing that with my parents, I thought.

I didn't know it at the time, but my dad had said exactly the same thing to my younger sister Pari, but she had got away with not going because she was in love with and living with Anthony.

My other sister Sarita had already moved to Canada with her husband Jack several years ago. She was a medical rep and was able to get a visa easily because of her job and transfer with her company. My brother in law Jack had previously been a Cadbury's Rep but had now bought a bar in Toronto, Canada. He would run it and we would sometimes go in there to play poole and have lunch.

So the three of us; me, my mum and my dad had rented a condo, which had a swimming pool on the ground floor. We would go swimming every day, then get ready, have breakfast and then walk into the town centre which was a five minute walk from us. We would have fruit smoothies every day and generally just walk around and then come back and watch films if we wanted. We had already done most of the main attractions in Toronto when we first got there; Niagra falls and the CN tower. The year went by in a blur. We never travelled the world like my dad had envisaged for us, as he had somehow lost all the money we were supposed to have to take with us. Plus I couldn't get a teaching job there as there were never any vacancies. Unlike in the U.K., teachers in Canada would stay in the same job until the end of their career. They have three months off over the summer and have a lot less work to do in the evenings and weekends as they just reuse what is already there. For some reason, in the U.K., teachers are made to plan everything from scratch every year and schemes of work are continually being changed. This is why there are over 100 recruitment agencies for teachers and there are hundreds of supply teachers needed to cover absence for teachers off with stress. I think some of these agencies earn more than teachers. Crazy!!! Anyway, to cut a long story short, I fell in love again … with a guy called Tashan. He was a friend of my brother in law's. It didn't end well. I always fuck up by getting too eager when I like someone. I thought I would never make the same mistakes again, especially after being so badly burnt the first time … but I always do.

Chapter 14 – London Life

January 2009

I am moving to London, after having lived in Canada for over a year. After a fresh heartbreak, moving somewhere vibrant and exciting is just what the doctor ordered. For the next nine years, I will live here and experience so many new things. I am free and the world is my oyster. Even though, I don't save any money or find the love of my life, I am content. I have two jobs; I work as a Supply Teacher and a Part time Charity Fundraiser. I am happy, as despite having two jobs, I don't feel overworked or suffocated like I did when I was teaching in a long term capacity in one school. Plus, there is so much politics in schools, that it becomes stressful and a serious headache. I love the teaching part, but there is so much more to deal with; 14 hour days, lesson observations which are heavily criticized, working all weekend, pressure to meet deadlines for paperwork, difficult colleagues or Teaching Assistants, difficult kids, special needs, no sleep during the week as you are constantly thinking all night about what you need to do next.

Supply teaching is so much easier. You just go in and teach. The lessons are all prepared and all the worksheets printed off ready for your lessons. You get a full lunch break and after you have finished the marking, you can go home and there is nothing more to do. Plus you have the flexibility of choosing the days you want to work. I loved it. I also loved the charity fundraising. I got to meet people from all walks of life; actors, musicians, dancers, students etc, all people trying to earn a bit extra doing some part time work. My life was good. A few years after moving to London, I also did some Freelance Tv presenting and now have my own You Tube channel. I had enough money to survive and for some reason, unlike my parents wish for me to save, buy a house etc, have material things to show my worth, I never felt the need to earn more money than was necessary to live a happy and content life. I had a roof over my head, swim every day at the local gym, had delicious food to eat and massages which I got regularly. I had made a few good friends and thought at the time, I would live and die in London. I also realised that life is actually more peaceful when there's no one of the opposite sex that you're interested in. Yet why does the heart still crave love? I will never know the answer to this.

When I first moved to London, I lived with my friend Neelam, sharing a room with her in her hotel. It was a small room and she only had a single bed, but we made it work. I lived with her for approximately six weeks or so before I found a decent, affordable place to rent. I had met a guy called Amar, on a previous shopping trip to Oxford Street and so was excited about dating him too as the hotel was so close. It was funny how we had met. He was the manager of the shop and I asked to try on some clothes in the changing rooms.

"Can I see your ID please?" he said.

"What? You need to show your ID to use the changing room?" I asked, surprised. I had always been rather gullible, so got out my ID and showed him.

"No I was just joking, you don't really need to show your ID," he laughed.

"Oh" I laughed back. "I was thinking that was rather strange". I then tried on the clothes, feeling rather foolish for having fallen for it, but also very amused. He was funny. I then bought a few items and he joked about how he couldn't believe I had fallen for it. I left, but kept thinking about him as I went into other shops. I finally plucked up the courage and wrote down my name and number on a piece of paper and went back and gave it to him. "Call me sometime I said".

"Oh okay thanks", he replied. I couldn't believe I had just done that. We text for a few weeks after that, before we arranged to meet for drinks. He said he had invited his uncle and his uncles girlfriend to come too and would that be okay.

"No problem" I said, thinking nothing of it, but in retrospect, I probably should have insisted it just be me and him for a first drink.

We ended up going to pizza express for dinner, four of us. Amar was being his funny self and introduced me to his uncle and his Polish girlfriend. She was pretty, but didn't speak any English. Amar's uncle spent most of his time talking to me. We all had quite a bit to drink and then Amar's uncle suggested we go back to his place on Bond street. We got a taxi there. I don't think I realised quite how much I had to drink, because as soon as we got back to Amar's uncles house I puked up all over his clean, cream carpet.

''Get her in the shower'' said Amars uncle, while he started to clean up the puke. Amar got me undressed and into the shower within minutes. Amar's uncle kept coming in to ask Amar questions while I was showering. Then Amar popped a towel around me and put me into bed.

''Don't do anything with her, she's drunk'' I overheard her uncle saying.

''No of course not'' Amar said, before closing the bedroom door and snuggling in beside me. He held me all night and made no moves and I loved him for it.

The next morning, Amar was up early and informed me he had to go to work, but I could just stay in bed and leave when I was ready. He said to text him when I was up. He said my clothes were all washed and on the dresser.

''Ok thank you'' I said sleepily. I went back to sleep. Half an hour after Amar had left, I suddenly felt someone grabbing my hand and hauling me out of bed. It was Amar's uncle.

''What are you doing?'' I mumbled half asleep.

''Come on, you can come and lie in my bed'' he said. A few seconds later, he had tucked me up in his bed. Then a few seconds after that, I felt his body climb into bed beside me. His hands were suddenly all over me.

''I haven't been able to stop thinking about you all night. I had to take sleeping tablets to finally get to sleep,'' he admitted, as he groped my body.

''No please stop,'' I objected, appalled at what he was doing, on top of the fact that he was betraying his nephew.

''Maria I want you. I don't want the blonde girl. She's just a distraction. I want you, please just hold me. Amar doesn't have to know. He's just a boy, I'm a man. I am very rich and can look after you. I'll take you away on holidays. You won't have to ever pay for anything again,'' he insisted. ''Have you ever had a man go down on you?'' he said, excitedly.

''No'', I said, shocked. Plus I wasn't attracted to him in the slightest.

"Really? Let me show you", he urged, as he started to go down under the covers.

"No please stop" I screamed, as I quickly got out of bed and started putting on my clothes, before he could touch me again.

"What are you doing?" he said, clearly annoyed.

"I have to go home. I can't do this."

"Okay I'll drive you home", he said.

"No, I'll get taxi, honestly I'll be fine".

"No no, I'll drive you to the station at least as it's on my way to work," he insisted.

Fifteen minutes later, we were in his car. He spent the whole journey trying to convince me why I should dump Amar and give him a shot.

"Think about it", were his departing words, as he left. I quickly got out of the car and walked to Neelam's hotel. I told her what had happened that evening. "You need to tell Amar what happened", she said wisely.

"But it's his uncle. Won't he be upset".

"Yes, but he sexually harassed you. Amar needs to know".

I thought about it and knew she was right.

Chapter 15 – Sanjeev's email

May 2002

A day after having received Sanjeev's email and digesting the new information that he was missing me, I was finally ready to respond.

''Hi Sanjeev, I'm surprised to hear from you. I miss you too. Why did you get married if you didn't like her? I was shocked when my sister told me, but I thought you must be really happy. If you're miserable, why don't you come back? or do you want me to come and see you? Maria. xx'' I pressed send.

A few days later, I got a response. ''Hey Maria, so good to get a response from you. No, I don't like her at all. I wish I was married to you. I just did it to make my parents happy. Yes definitely come here. I would love to see you. I miss you sooo much Maria.''

I felt so happy that he was missing me and said he wished he was married to me. Once my PGCE was completed and I had passed, I booked a flight to LA. It cost £500, but my parents found out and made me cancel it. That didn't stop me from rebooking it and making up a lie that I was going to stay with my friend in London for two weeks. I think my parents suspected what I was up to, but they didn't say anything the second time. It was the most spontaneous and brave thing I had ever done up until that point. As I waited to board the plane, I felt excited and anxious to see Sanjeev again. I had booked a hotel for two weeks and arrived on Friday. As I unpacked my stuff, I emailed Sanjeev that I had arrived in Los Angeles and was looking forward to seeing him. He emailed back that he would be free to come and see me on the Sunday which was two days away. So I spent the next couple of days exploring Los Angeles and walking around the city.

When Sunday came round, Sanjeev picked me up from my hotel at 7pm as promised. He took me out for dinner. It was so strange seeing him again, but I knew how strongly I felt for him, as my heart was beating so fast. After dinner, we went back up to my hotel room and talked for a bit, but soon started kissing. It got passionate quite quickly and Sanjeev started trying to remove my clothes before I stopped him. "No. Sanjeev stop. I can't do this. It's not right. You're still married".

"But I don't love her or want her. I just married her for the green card, you know that.

"But you're still married and I don't want my first time to be like that". What Sanjeev said next cut me to my core.

"Wow... you're gonna be an old woman before you do it. By the way, I have cheated on my wife. My boss asked me to sleep with his wife."

"Does your wife not know?" I questioned.

"No."

Sanjeev then quickly put his jacket and shoes on and announced he was leaving. I sat on my bed in shock at what had just happened. Part of me was proud of the fact that I hadn't given in to temptation and slept with a married man just because I was deeply in love with him. The other part of me questioned whether Sanjeev was right. Would I be an old maid before I did it? The next day, I sent Sanjeev an email.

'Hi Sanjeev, will I see you again while I'm here in LA? I came all the way here just to see you and I'm here for two weeks. I'm sorry I couldn't sleep with you, but I believe that one day I will meet someone who will love and respect me for it. Maria'.

As I sent my email, I wondered whether that was true. Would I ever meet someone who would love and respect me for waiting and being a virgin for them or was Sanjeev right and I would die an old maid....

Sanjeev never replied to my email, even though I kept checking it every few hours for the next few days. I knew he wasn't coming out to see me again, even though I had flown thousands of miles just to see him. I was devastated. I spent the next few days just going out to eat alone and walking around the city. After a week of doing this and feeling lonelier every day, I finally broke down and went to the staff in the hotel reception. I told them what had happened and although my stay was supposed to be for two weeks,

I wanted to leave a week earlier. I sobbed my heart out to the staff and they were amazing. They called the airport staff and got me a flight booked for the next day at no extra cost. I went back to my room and packed. The next day I was travelling back to the UK on an eight hour flight. This trip had cost me £1000 all in the name of love. Was it worth it? The stupid things we all do for love!

Chapter 16 – The Gatehouse School

Nov 2005

I have been teaching at The Gatehouse school for three months now. It is an EBD school. EBD stands for emotional and Behavioural difficulties. It is basically an all boys school for 12 to 18 year olds who have been expelled from mainstream schools for disruptive, inappropriate or violent behaviour. These children often have severe emotional and behavioural problems for various reasons. My task is to try and help them get back into mainstream schools, by understanding where they are coming from. I teach English, Computing and Art to small classes with about 6 or 7 children at a time. It can be difficult, especially as some of these children will often just run out of class or get into physical fights with each other, or as I am soon to find out, make inappropriate remarks. I have to find a way to make learning fun and enjoyable and keep them focused. All of the other teachers are very supportive of each other and one teacher in particular called James Harvey is always coming in to help me tidy up in the classroom at the end of the day.

One day I'm in the classroom, teaching Art to a class of 7 boys. One of them asks for help on how to get the proportions right for the portrait drawings. I go to assist when suddenly one of the other boys grabs his hand and puts it on my breast.

'Alex that's not appropriate is it?" I say sternly. The boys all start to snigger at their desks. I move away and carry on helping the other boys. Once one child has finished their portrait and painted it, they put it on the rack to dry and then go off their cooking lesson. I am left with one boy in the class; a tall boy called Jackson. He finishes his Art work and puts it on the rack to dry. Once he washes his hands, he joins me at the teacher desk, as I am just finishing off some paperwork. Suddenly, I feel something metal against the side of my forehead. "Will you go out with me Miss?", Jackson says with a staple gun pressed against my forehead. Too stunned to respond immediately, I wait a few seconds to quickly gather my thoughts. "ummm yeah maybe", I stutter, with my heart beating rapidly inside my chest. Being someone with a low pain threshold, I can't think of a worse predicament to be in.

"Maybe", repeats Jackson back to me.

"I'll think about it, but first you need to go to your cooking lesson."

Jackson doesn't move and keeps the staple gun pressed up against my head. My heart is beating so fast and I can feel my palms getting sweaty. I look towards the door to see if anyone is walking past that can notice what's going on and come and help me. After what seems like an eternity, Mrs. Brown, my teaching assistant pokes her head through the door. Relief floods my body.

''Hi I was just coming to ask you what day you want me to book the ICT suite for our English lesson next week. The times available are on this list,'' says Mrs. Brown.

''Oh that's great. Let me come and have a look'', I say and slowly move towards the door and away from Jackson. I go outside of the door and pretend to look at the sheet in her hands, as I whisper and tell her my situation. ''What am I going to do?'' I whisper to her.

''Don't worry. I am going to get the keys and we will need to lock him in the classroom'', she whispers back. She walks quietly and confidently to where the keys are kept and is back in a matter of seconds and then silently locks the door and informs me that she will go to get help and get one of the male teachers to deal with Jackson. I am so grateful to her and say thank you.

''You're welcome. Go and take a breather in the staff room and you will need to write all this down on one of the incident forms'', she says to me kindly.

''Okay I will''. I walk to the staffroom and make myself a cup of tea and relax for a few minutes, before recording everything down. Wow! This job is going to be harder than I thought, I think to myself as I realise what serious danger I had just escaped from. Luckily the next few weeks go without any major incidents, but a month later, I am faced with another situation, which I probably should have dealt with more severely. I am teaching Shakespeare in English and I put on video which shows a scene in which the main actress is getting groped against her will, by one of the actors. A few of the boys start commenting.

''Is he raping her?'' another comments.

''I want to rape Miss'' another child called Alex suddenly says.

I looked at him. Did he just say that? I was too stunned to speak and didn't know how to react. He looked back at me and I could tell he was unsure whether I had overheard him. I let the video continue until the end and didn't mention it, as I didn't know how to react. Looking back, I probably should have taken him outside the classroom and had a quiet word with him about the comment. At least that was what my cousin said I should have done when I relayed the incident to him one weekend over a cup of tea. He was right, but I think I had been too shocked to respond at the time. Another incident that really stands out during my time at The Gatehouse school, was during a Computing lesson with the boys. They were meant to be doing a project on a topic of their choice, but instead were all watching porn on the internet.

''Boys you need to be doing your project work, you need to come off that now'', I said firmly. The boys completely ignored me and carried on watching porn. The Teaching Assistant and I looked at each other.

"I'll go and get Mr. Williams", she said to me. Mr. Williams was the Assistant Headteacher and also taught Science in the school. Five minutes later, she was back with him.

"Boys get off that now! You all know you are supposed to be doing your project work", shouted Mr. Williams in a loud, booming voice.

"What do you mean? You were in here with us the other day watching porn too," announced one of the boys, looking directly at Mr. Williams. Mr. Williams turned bright red, while the TA and I looked at each other and tried to contain our laughter.

Chapter 17 – It's over!

August 2021

It is completely finished with Mark. I was sending him lots of messages and he has just been ignoring them. Yesterday, I sent him one final message, saying there's no point in continuing when we rarely see each other and there's no communication. He didn't reply once again and so I deleted him. It's a shame as we lived so close to each other, like a fifteen minute drive. Long distance relationships don't work as far as I'm concerned as you can't create a bond if you rarely see each other and I hate travelling. So do guys I've discovered. No one wants to make an effort anymore. Mark lived so close and still didn't make an effort. After having deleted Tinder, Bumble and Hinge twice this summer already, I have come back on again. I only have a week left of my summer holidays and will be back at work teaching again at my new school in Peterborough on the 1st. I know I won't have any time to date once I start back, so I was trying to fit in all the dates now, but doesn't seem to be working out. The other problem I have is my flatmates. Three of them are in their fifties and they have implemented a million house rules. I'm not sure why people in their fifties are even living in a house share as they are so intolerant of other people at that age. Plus I have another problem now with Jonathon, who keeps making sexual innuendo's towards me and the other day he took it all one step too far, when he came up behind me and pressed himself up against me while I was cooking. I was shocked as I could feel his hardness against me and I cried out "Jonathon, what are you doing?" He played the innocent card and was like "What happened?" I need to move out pronto and have asked my landlord if there are any other houses I could move to, that will be nearer my new job.

Chapter 18 – London Life

February 2009

'Your uncle sexually harassed me last night', I told Amar over the phone, once I had finally plucked up the courage to call him.

'What? I can't believe you're saying that. That is my uncle', replied Amar and then put the phone down. I was shaking. He didn't believe me. A few minutes later, he called me back. 'Tell me what happened,' he said.

''I thought you didn't believe me''.

''I was joking. I know what my uncle is like. He's done that before'', he laughed.

''It's not funny Amar. After you left, your uncle came into the bedroom and dragged me out of bed and said I could sleep in his bed. Then he got in beside me and started touching me.''

''Did you sleep with him?'' he asked.

''Of course not. I quickly got out of bed and started putting my clothes on. He was saying he couldn't get me out of his head all night''.

''Yeah he kept coming in while you were showering. Sorry are you ok?''

"Yeah I will be, but you need to tell him to stop texting me, as he has sent me like a million messages".

"Ok don't worry. Look I'll see you soon okay," and then he put the phone down.

I don't know what happened between Amar and his uncle, but after that Amar didn't text me or ask me out again. After a week of waiting, I sent him a message saying "I don't think it's a good idea for us to see each other again, because your uncle keeps leaving me voice messages and texting me constantly". I think in my head I was rejecting him before he could reject me and I was hoping he would then fight for me and beg me to not leave him. The plan backfired. He just text me "okay". I then tried to back track, but he stopped replying to any of my messages. I then went a bit crazy and kept walking past his shop, until one day when he was actually in. I went straight up to him and was like "Amar why are you ignoring all my messages?" in a panicked, loud voice, in front of all his customers. He grabbed my arm and was like "let's talk outside". He smiled and was like "you look nice".

"Thank you", I replied, "but why are you ignoring me?" I cried.

"Because you ended it. I'm not gonna beg someone".

''You don't have to beg. I'm yours,'' I replied, sincerely. Little did I know that this is the worst thing you can say to a guy in the early stages of dating. It scares a man.

''aah'', he said. ''Look I need to go back into the shop as we're busy today. I'll text you later okay''.

''Okay'' I answered. I never heard from him again and he never replied to any of my messages after that.

What was I doing wrong when it came to dating? I always seemed to fuck things up before they even started. LOL

Chapter 19 – Sanjeev returns

December 2002

More than six months had passed since Sanjeev had broken my heart for the second time in LA. I had come back and remember thinking how I had a lucky escape. The other part of me also wondered if I would ever find someone who I could feel the way I had felt about Sanjeev. Normal life resumed though. I had passed my PGCE and was applying for teaching jobs.

One cold December evening, I got a text from Sanjeev's old phone number. 'Hey I'm back in the UK. How are you? Sanjeev'.

I sat in shock. This was unexpected. Confusing. I did not think I would ever hear from him again. I didn't reply for at least a couple of weeks and had no intention of ever speaking to him again after how he had treated me when I had gone to LA. But the other part of me felt alone, as there was no one else and I often wondered if I would ever love again. I replied to his message after exactly two weeks. "I'm good thanks. You?" I kept it short on purpose. "Yeah good thanks. It's nice to be back. Fancy catching up over a drink?" replied Sanjeev.

"Why? Is there any point?" I countered back.

''Yeah I think there's a point. I'm sorry about LA, but I'm not the same person anymore, so I think it's worth giving it a second shot'', he responded.

Against my better judgement, I agreed to give him another chance. I got a cousin of mine, Mindy to join us and he said he would bring a friend along to. We met in Moon under Water in Milton Keynes and went onto a club after. I was feeling nervous as we entered the bar. I'm not sure how the rest of the evening went exactly, but I remember Mindy mentioning how good looking he was. I remember having a drink and going onto the club. I remember Sanjeev's friend having broken English, having recently come over from India. I remember dancing as a group, but trying not to let Sanjeev get to close to me. Then I remember sitting down at a table, with Sanjeev next to me and feeling excited and nervous having him sit so close next to me. We left shortly after and I dropped Mindy home.

A few weeks later, Sanjeev was having a leaving do for someone at his work and invited me to join. I went but when I got there, he treated me like shit! (I guess leopards rarely change their spots! Lol) He proceeded to flirt with every girl at the venue in front of me and more or less ignored me for most of the evening. What happened next is a blur…. Which I have done my best to forget!! Basically, we went back to his and we tried to have sex, but we couldn't the first time as I was too tight. ''I might as well have got some other girl'', he said coldly. ''How can you say that?' I cried. We never saw each other again after that!!! What an idiot I had been! To ever think that was love!

Chapter 20 – Drifting

March 2022

I feel like I'm drifting. Every day is the same and I'm not sure what to do. I applied to be a prison officer and after passing the first 2 online assessments, it kept saying no slots available when I tried to book a virtual interview and then suddenly said I could no longer continue with the application. Trying to get back into presenting again but it's not easy. Doing supply teaching again and although much easier than a long term role, its not what I want anymore.

I went on a date with a guy called Ashley at beginning of December. We met in London Bridge which was halfway between us. I lived in St. Neots and he was in Welling. I wouldn't have reached out to him to meet if I hadn't been trying to get Jonathon off my back. Jonathon (my 50 year old flatmate) was constantly touching me and making dirty jokes. I guess I needed someone hot to finally get him off my case, which was why I messaged Ashley on facebook. Ashley had ghosted me 4 years prior to that when we had first started messaging, but then when we were supposed to go on our first date, he suddenly disappeared and we never met. I guess I should have known from that he was clearly a popular guy who got a lot of attention from women and probably didn't need me, but it absolutely worked in getting Jonathon off my back.

We arranged to meet in London Bridge. I wore a black dress and black boots. I saw Joanna (a friend of my cousins) on the train there. She looked amazing and is now a millionaire at only 37 years old and owns 2 houses. She hardly has to work now. So lucky. It was a nice old catch up and she walked me to the station entrance. I could see Ashley so I hugged her and said Goodbye. I walked across the road to where he was standing. We walked to a nearby pub and sat outside as there was a fire burning and Covid rules still applied. He bought the first round. I had a prosecco and he got a beer. I knew straight away I fancied him, but never give anything away, mainly because I don't know how to flirt. We'd been chatting for an hour, when the waiter came over and asked if we wanted another drink. "No, I'm okay" I said.

"I'll have another beer" said Ashley.

"Actually, I'll have another prosecco too then", I said, not wanting to appear rude and letting him drink alone. He then started chatting to the waiter. "Shall I get this one?" I mumbled, but he was chatting to waiter, so I just got out my card and paid. I had asked him out for a drink, so felt like I should anyway.

"What accent has the waiter got?" I asked Ashley.

"Birmingham". I impersonated the Birmingham accent and Ashley copied me. "I don't really like the Birmingham accent", I laughed.

We then continued to chat for another hour and as I noticed Ashley get his phone out to check a message perhaps, I then announced that I had to go home now. I had been with him a couple of hours now and I always think the first date should be short and sweet. As we said our goodbyes at the station, he looked like he wasn't sure whether to kiss me and he went close to my mouth, but I offered my cheek instead. It was a first date after all. I then got on my train and got a text message from him a few minutes later. "Did you get on the train okay?"

"Yes thanks for a fun date", I replied.

"It was cool. Second date?" he text back.

"Yeah second date sounds like a plan", I responded. However, a second date never happened. He clearly had lots of other options closer to home.

Chapter 21 – Presenting opportunity

October 2012

I had been working at the charity place and supply teaching for a few years now in London. I loved my life as it was mostly stress free. I decided that I was sick of teaching and wanted to try my hand at Television presenting. I was often told I had a beautiful speaking voice and am clear and engaging. So I asked my good friend Will at the time, if he could help me make a showreel by videoing me doing some presenting. He agreed and this was to be the start of my short-lived presenting journey.

One cool evening, I invited Will over to make my video. I had a script ready and after a few takes, we had it perfected. It was now ready to go on You Tube and be emailed to lots of TV producers. I sent it to Blue Peter and lots of other channels. However, I didn't hear back from anyone. I then got in touch with people who worked in TV on Linked in and sent them messages. However, apart from one or two replies with tips on how to get into the business, I didn't get any job offers at this time. A couple of years later, when I made a second (and much more professional) showreel with the producers of X factor and Big Brother, I did get work for an Asian channel called B4U and actually ended up getting some freelance work with them presenting for a few shows. I loved it, but it is a really difficult industry to get into mainstream and make a career from as it so competitive.

Anyway, back to December 2012, a couple of months after I had made my first showreel, I was approached at work by a new colleague who had recently joined Pell and Bales. This was the charity fundraising place I worked at Part time to supplement my supply teaching. His name was Farhid. He was a short, Muslim guy who I noticed staring at me a few times.

'Hi, I'm Farhid. I watched your presenting showreel and was really impressed' he said to me one day, when we were on a break from calls.

'Oh thank you' I replied.

'I'm actually looking for a presenter to front a charity I've recently set up called Mirror Mirror, which is helping people who suffer from Body dysmorphic disorder' he continued, excitedly.

'Oh that's great. Tell me more. What is Body dysmorphic disorder?' I asked.

'It's basically when people look in the mirror and they seem a deformed version of themselves. Over 2 million people suffer from it worldwide. Leah Walker from Big Brother wrote a book about it, as she suffered from it all her life' he continued. 'Google it. There's a lot written about it'.

'I will'.

'Here. Take my number and give me yours. Let's stay in touch and I'll keep you informed with when I need you to present for my charity and interview people suffering with it' he stated confidently.

'Ok great' I replied.

That evening, I went home and researched all about Body Dysmorphic disorder and all the information he had given me to check that what he was saying was true. It was. So over the next few evenings, I wrote lots of questions I could ask potential interviewees about this disorder. I also wrote a long introduction about what BDD was, so I could explain it when filming.

The next time I was working at Pell and Bales was a couple of days later and Farid came and sat down next to me. In between calls, he would make casual conversation with me about things and I got a weird vibe. My instinct was telling me something was off about him and this only got stronger when he would continue to come and sit next to me at work and ask me lots of questions which had nothing to do with what he had initially proposed to me. He also started sending me text messages asking me if I cooked Indian food and when was I going to cook for him and lots of other messages completely unrelated to the presenting. After several messages from him like this and one where he was asking me if I was a naughty girl, I finally got sick of it and messaged him back something like this **'Hi Farid, I'm afraid I'm a good** *girl. Always have been. Always will be. I'd appreciate it if you stuck to work related messages from now on. I don't appreciate all these messages which have nothing to do with presenting, especially as that was the reason you asked for my number. I would not have given my number had I known that you might have a different motive. Thank you. Mina.'*

I was sick of his messages and had been feeling really uncomfortable for a while whenever he came and sat next to me at work. Plus I wasn't it the least bit attracted to him and I had the feeling he had ulterior motives from his behaviour and messages.

He responded immediately. *'My apologies. I didn't mean to offend you. From now on, I will only approach you with work related messages and be in touch when you are needed for the presenting. Farid.'*

I started having my suspicions and serious doubts about this whole thing, so went to ask my main boss, Darren Gorman, if he could find out if Mirror Mirror was a genuine charity. He said if the charity was still in the early days and going through the process of registration, he wouldn't know. Farid had said it was going through the process of registration, so that didn't help me. I then asked my line manager, Simon and he also said he didn't know. I had lots of friends at Pell and Bales and everyone there seemed to love me for some reason, which was a pleasant experience as I had spent most of my youth as a loner, as you already know. One friend in particular called Sharlene was someone I felt I could confide in, so I went and told her my doubts.

'Right, don't worry. I'm going to question him in detail. If he's made the whole thing up, I will find out and I will beat the crap out of him! Don't worry hun. I've got your back,' she said to me reassuringly. I laughed out loud. She had balls this girl. Half an hour later, after having thoroughly interrogated him, she returned to my side.

'Right girl, I think he's genuine. He went into quite a lot of detail and I don't think you can make that all up', she said confidently.

'Ok thanks Sharlene, I appreciate it', I replied and gave her a hug, but I still had this strange niggling feeling …… call it a women's intuition!

Chapter 22 – Salsa

July 2014

'Injustice anywhere is a threat to justice everywhere. We are caught in and inescapable network of mutuality, tied in a single garment of destiny. Whatever affects one directly, affects us all indirectly''.

Martin Luther King

While we were working at Pell and Bales, raising money for charities, my good friend Ellie suggested doing something fun and trying Salsa dancing. She said there were some great places we could get Salsa lessons. I really liked the idea as needed to inject some fun and excitement into my life. We both googled the best places to learn and found Abacus bar in London Bridge had great reviews. Plus it wasn't too far too travel from Old street where we worked. We planned to go once a week on a Tuesday during the summer holidays and work our afternoon shift till 5.30pm and then grab a bite to eat, before heading over to Abacus bar around 7ish. The class was starting at 7.30pm. So we started one Tuesday evening in late July. It was a warm evening and we had worn dresses and heels for our first beginners lesson. There was a lady called Maria (same name as me) who was the teacher of the beginners group. We all formed around her in a large circle and she started by showing us some simple steps to copy. There was around 16 of us. There was a surprising number of men that were learning too. The lesson was an hour long and Maria patiently guided us through lots of basic steps for us to copy and learn. We had a chance to repeat the steps until we got them and Maria would come and support anyone who was struggling. After the hour was up, everyone got to mingle and talk to other teachers and other dancers. There was salsa music and everyone could ask other partners to dance with them. I liked this bit as meant you could practice your steps in a more relaxed atmosphere and with more advanced dancers. Ellie and I stood near the back of the dance hall to chat.

"That was really fun" I said to Ellie.

"Yeah it was. I definitely wanna keep coming", Ellie replied.

"Yeah me too. That guy over there is really attractive, don't you think?" I whispered in Ellie's ear.

"Oh yeah. He's not my type though. I think he's one of the instructors", she replied.

"Oh really. How do you know?"

"I'm sure I saw him teaching the other group".

"Aah ok. I need the toilet. Will you come with me?"

"Yeah sure".

There were 4 groups at salsa; beginners, improvers, intermediate and advanced. It would be good to get to advanced I thought to myself. I went to the toilet and redid my lipstick and Ellie did the same, before we both went back into the salsa room. We had only been back in the room less than a minute before the attractive guy I had been talking about suddenly approached us. He came up to me and smiled ''Hi. I'm Newton. Are you enjoying yourself?''

''Yeah it's really fun.'' I replied with a smile back.

''What do you do?'' he asked.

''I'm a teacher''.

''Wow, beauty as well as brains!'' he complimented me.

''Thank you'', I beamed.

''Would you like a dance?''

''Yeah okay.''

He grabbed my hand and walked me to the middle of the dance floor.

Over the next few weeks, we continued to go to Salsa and Newton gave me his number and said if I wanted private lessons, he could help me develop further. I messaged him and we were texting and talking on the phone frequently. I remember one such phone call where he said 'I don't understand why an intelligent, beautiful woman like you is single'. I laughed and said 'I don't know either, but I seem to attract idiots'. Soon after, we went for dinner.

It wasn't until the sixth time I went to Salsa, that the incident happened. My friend Ellie was ill this time and so couldn't come, but she urged me to go anyway, so I did. Newton had just finished his class with us, when I bumped into him at the entrance. We started to chat, when I went to kiss him.

'No no I can't do that you know' he whispered. 'My girlfriend's standing over there you know'. Shocked at this sudden announcement, I looked over his shoulder to see an average looking woman with shoulder length hair gazing over at us. 'Don't worry, I'll talk to you later', he said quickly, before rushing off to where his girlfriend was standing by the bar. Wow!! I walked off in daze, caught the underground train and went home. Men! Why did he not say that from the start rather than giving me his number, calling me multiple times on the phone for chats and taking me out for dinner?? Instead, he used the fact that I was attracted to him, he was my teacher and led me on to think there was the possibility of more.

I called my friend Ellie and told her what had happened. 'What a dickhead!' she said. 'Men can be such pigs. Don't let this put you off salsa though!'

'No I wasn't going to' I responded.

The following week, we went to salsa as normal, but I noticed that his girlfriend was there. She kept her eyes peeled on him the whole time. This happened the following week too, until one day I got a text message from him saying I had been banned from salsa. It was a strange message to receive on my mobile, basically saying that due to unwanted advances made by me, I was banned from salsa. Shocked and outraged, I showed my friend Ellie.

'What the fuck? That message has come from his girlfriend', she declared, clearly outraged on my behalf. 'What are you gonna do? I think we should still go!'

'I completely agree. I'm not letting someone tell me that I can't go salsa when I've done absolutely nothing wrong!' I shouted passionately. 'It's ridiculous and unjust'. So the next week we went to salsa as normal. When we got inside, I went directly to the manager and asked him 'Can I ask you Tony, have I been banned from salsa?'

'Of course not Maria, you're one of our best students. Why would you think that?' Tony replied.

I looked at my friend Ellie and she gave me a knowing smile. 'I told you Maria. That message came from Newton's girlfriend. She clearly feels threatened by you'.

Angry and resolute, I walked into the salsa class. Newton suddenly saw me and appeared unaffected, although I could tell he was shocked inside by my rebellious appearance and complete disregard for his text. 'Aah you made it' he said casually, as I walked past.

'Yeah I did', I replied, with my head held high. Ellie and I walked into the centre of the hall, as Newton announced for everyone to form a huge circle.

Chapter 23 – Gorwood Primary School

February 2023

Wow! So much to talk about. A toxic headteacher, great colleagues and a crush on the Assistant Headteacher! What am I doing? This is not easy. Every time I think my story is nearly over, life proves me wrong. But this school has kind of brought me to life again in a weird way. I was seriously depressed last summer and having anxiety issues the night before I started at this school. Little did I know, Stacey who started at the same time as me, had been feeling the same way. Is there a reason I've been brought back to this school? I was meant to start here before Covid started, but then Covid started and they didn't need me. Anyway, I thought it would be a nice feeling to have a crush on a colleague and in some ways it is, in that I feel alive again, but on the other hand, he has a girlfriend and so it's really annoying and difficult! I get the vibe he fancies me too as since the start, he's sought me out to talk to me and was helping me constantly with Computing stuff and PE stuff. Although that could just be because he's being a nice guy. But I also noticed he would often blush while talking to me and not with others. Men I've spoken to say this is because he's aroused by me, while women say I shouldn't read much into that, as it could mean nothing. My instinct is that it does mean something, but I have been wrong before.

Anyways, I think he's a lot younger than me, even though he is the assistant head. He must know by now my actual age as news seems to travel fast around this school. It's a small school and this was my biggest fear. That I would be exposed in a larger school and people would get to know the "real me" and discover how strange and weird I am. However, everyone has been really nice and has accepted me just the way I am …. Unless they're being fake and bad mouthing me behind my back. You never know who you can trust … even people you think would never betray or lie to you .. can and have. I've cut many people out over the years.

On my first day at Gorwood, I remember being so scared. It was a warmish day and we had 2 training days to start with. I spoke to everyone. I already knew the assistant head Ben Thompson was a good looking guy from having met him back when I came in for an interview and he was one of the most welcoming people to the school. "Help yourself to tea or coffee" he had said to me back then. "Thank you. I'm ok though as I've got my water".

"How's your day going?" he enquired.

"It's good. I've just had a tour and test and now waiting for the interview" I replied.

"Aah okay well good luck", he said and smiled pleasantly.

''Thank you. Any plans for the summer?'' I asked casually.

''I've got my brother's wedding in Ireland'', he responded.

''Aah nice. I had 3 weddings last year, but Indian weddings are a nightmare as they last for 5 days and there always ends up being arguments of some sort''.

''I've never been to an Indian wedding before''.

''You're not missing out''.

Suddenly, the door opened and in stepped the office manager. ''You can go in for your interview now Miss. Bassett''.

''Aah thank you'' I said as I started walking towards the door with my bag.

''Good luck'' called out Mr. Thompson as I walked past him.

''Thank you'' I smiled at him.

I didn't think much of this exchange to be honest at the time. I knew he was good looking and very welcoming, but that was it. Over the summer, I did think about him from time to time and it was nice knowing that I'd have an attractive male colleague to work with, which is rare in Primary schools, but mostly I enjoyed my holiday to Crete with my mum and sister and put him to the back of my mind. I felt depressed when I got back from Crete and my plan to get fit over the summer didn't really happen. I just stayed in bed and watched films for most of it. My only exercise was swimming or cleaning. On my first day in, I was so scared, but having met a few of the colleagues over the summer; Michela, Tegan and Bill, it did help a little. I walked into the training room for the first day, having already said hello to a few of my colleagues and the first two people I saw was Ben and Jim sitting at the back of the room. I smiled broadly from one to the other. Ben smiled back but Jim looked down at the table and didn't seem to want to make eye contact with me. I later realised that it takes him time to warm up to people. I quickly sat down at the table at the front and started talking to Harriet who was one of the teachers I hadn't met yet. I introduced myself and found out she was married to a guy who was a manager of the Escape rooms in Peterborough. I found her really interesting. She was also pregnant and due to have the baby at the end of the year.

A short while later, the headteacher and Deputy walked in. The headteacher asked me to join Michela and Tegan's table, which was fine because I'd already met them over the summer, when I came in to help Michella set up the classroom.

During a break on the training day, I made some idle chat with my new colleagues, Tegan and Michella. ''What are your tattoo's of?''

''My children's names and birthdays'', replied Michella.

''Aah that's nice as it means something. What about you Tegan?''

'' I've got a heart'', said Tegan.

''I'd love to get a tattoo, but I don't like needles. I think I'd have to go to Las vegas and get really drunk to get one'', I stated.

Michella and Tegan chuckled at my comment.

Later during the term, I discovered they were both really fun and had lots of naughty and flirty banter with the men in the school. Well actually I had only heard them be naughty with Bill, the caretaker. Apart from Bill, there were two other men, Ben and Jim, but I don't think they would do that with Jim, as he was married to the headteacher. Ben had a girlfriend, but I'm sure they probably had done that with him in the past, although I hadn't heard it.

I'm now on half term and being really lazy and unproductive. Had a car accident. Nightmare!!

Chapter 24 – Presenting con

February 2013

It was about six weeks later that I got the phone call at 11pm at night. After Sharlene had reassured me that Farid was telling the truth, I continued to do more research for the Mirror Mirror project and was really excited to start my first real presenting project. I had just put on my pyjama's and was getting ready for bed, when my phone rang, but I didn't recognise the number.

'Hello, is this Maria?' asked the unfamiliar female voice on the other end.

'Yes it is', I replied.

'Hi. I'm Farid's girlfriend and I'm just wondering who you are, as I've seen lots of messages between you and my boyfriend?'

'Yeah it was purely professional. Your boyfriend approached me at work about two months ago, offering me a job to present for his new charity called Mirror Mirror'.

'Mirror Mirror? Yeah he was working for them, but that charity went into dissolution about three months ago.'

I couldn't believe what I was hearing. I could feel the rage building inside me.

'Whhatt!! Sweetheart ……. You're fucking bastard boyfriend made up a whole load of shit just to get my number. How fucking dare he!!! What a bloody ……' Before I could continue with my rant, she quickly passed the phone to Farid. 'Hear … speak to Farid.'

'Farid, you fucking cunt. How dare you…' I shouted down the phone.

'Listen, my girlfriend doesn't know what she's talking about. She's …..'

Before he could continue with his lies, I slammed the phone down on him. I was seething with fury! I had wasted the last two months doing research and preparing questions for what!!! Nothing but lies!! That night I couldn't sleep. I was still angry when I got into work the next day. I went straight to my manager, Darren.

'Darren have you got a minute?'

'Yeah sure', he replied.

'Do you remember I asked you if you could find out about that charity called Mirror Mirror? Well I just found out last night from the guys girlfriend that he made the whole thing up. If I see him, I'm going to hit him, but I can appreciate you don't want any violence in the workplace', I said as calmly as I could. I noticed a slight smile creep onto my manager's face as I said this.

'Oh does he work here?'

'Yes. His name is Farid'.

'Okay don't worry, I'll deal with it. Maybe just keep away from him', Darren advised.

'Thank you. Yeah ok', I replied and walked off to a seat near some friends.

News spreads fast. Over the next few days, I told Sharlene what happened and when a few others asked me what was happening with the presenting thing I had been excited about, I told them the truth. Soon everyone seemed to know and were giving Farid the cold shoulder. It wasn't long before he left. My gut instinct had been right all along! In future, following my gut instinct got me out of many scrapes I'm sure. That and prayer. God is truly great and the fact that I'm still alive despite all the challenges I have faced in my life prove at least to me, that there is indeed a god. A god who loves me despite all my many flaws. Thank you God.

Chapter 25 – Salsa injustice continued

August 2014

The music started and Newton chose a student to help him demonstrate some of the salsa moves that he wanted us to learn with a partner. Then we had to move round the circle and practice with each person around the circle. After a couple of minutes of this, Newton who was standing in the centre of the circle, would also select students from the circle and pull them into the centre to dance with him. I thought he might not choose me, due to guilt for what he had done, but then he did. He pulled me in close to him and said 'you're really improving by the way'.

'Thank you' I said simply and continued to be led in the dance. I remembered a previous lesson when he had pulled me into the middle, before his girlfriend had found out and he had proceeded to grind up against me so I could feel his hardness protruding against me, thick and stiff. Then he had moved me back to the circle. Was that professional for an instructor to be pressing their erect manhood against a student, let alone one who had a girlfriend? Once the lesson was over, Ellie and I left and went home.

'I'm proud of you', said Ellie to me.

'Thank you Ellie. I'm proud of myself too'.

The following week, Ellie was ill again and couldn't attend, but she urged me to still go, so I went as normal. However, I wasn't expecting what happened next. I got to the salsa venue and was met at the front desk by the manager Tony, who had only last week told me I wasn't banned.

'I'm sorry, you can't come in Maria. You've been banned'.

'What? Why?' I countered back, aghast.

'Newton', he replied.

'But I haven't done anything wrong. You told me last week that I hadn't been banned'.

'Yes but Newton said you've been pursuing and harassing him.'

'What?? That's crazy and a total lie! And I've got numerous messages on my phone from him to me, that prove that he was the one pursuing me', I shouted back emotionally. I could feel the tears building up at the injustice of it all! 'You can have a look on my phone. He pursued me. Why do I need to chase a man that doesn't want me? I'm not being arrogant, but I don't need to'. I could now feel the tears streaming down my face.

'I know. I believe you, but I still can't let you in as Newton's girlfriend is very upset by all this!', replied Tony. Wow Wow Wow!!!

'How do you think I feel, when I've done nothing wrong? I'm gonna go to all the papers and say that innocent people get banned from salsa!' I was really screaming now and people turned to look at us.

'I'm sorry' said Tony calmly and simply.

I realised there was no point in me standing here and arguing, so I walked away and went home. I told Ellie what had happened and she was as shocked as me. I never went back to salsa again after that and prayed that Karma would work it's magic. However, I still couldn't resist sending a message to Newton as I was furious with rage. 'I cannot believe you have lied and got me banned, when you and I both KNOW I have done nothing wrong Newton!' I text him in a fit of rage!!'

'Maria this needs to STOP. I have warned you not to cross the line and you have ignored the warnings!' Wow! This was laughable. Clearly his girlfriend was beside him as he sent the message.

'What needs to stop? You pursuing me and grinding up against me in salsa lessons?' I replied back. No response came back. Clearly him and his girlfriend must be having an argument about what I had just messaged him.

Once I got home, I took my make up off and got straight into bed. I thought that was the end of the whole saga, but a few days later, I got a phone call from Newton's girlfriend. 'Hi. Is that Maria?' she said.

'Yes it is', I replied.

'Newton has told me everything that's happened and I think you've been really disrespectful, considering you knew he had a girlfriend.'

'What... that's completely untrue. Newton NEVER told me had a girlfriend. I didn't find out till much later and I found out by accident', I argued back.

'You're lying', she spat back angrily.

'No I'm not. It's the truth,' I replied.

'Well we're moving in together soon, so you need to leave him alone or I'll get the police involved', she shouted down the phone.

'I'm not chasing him. He's been chasing me', I shouted back. 'And good luck with moving in together. Every time you don't know where he is or can't get hold of him, you'll be wondering who he's with and what he's doing. You clearly don't trust him.'

'How dare you tell me how to behave with my boyfriend', she screamed and slammed the phone down. Clearly I'd hit a nerve.

A few days later, I had a missed call from a number I didn't recognise. They had left a voicemail. 'Hello Miss. Bassett. This is PC Bates calling from Lewisham police station. Could you please call me back as a matter of urgency on this number. Thank you'.

I had some food and called back an hour later.

'Hello. Could I speak to PC Bates please? I had a voice message on my phone to call her back ASAP'.

'PC Bates speaking. Thank you for calling me back. I've had a complaint from a Mr. Newton Barnes of sexual harassment by yourself'.

'That's a lie', I state matter of factly. 'Newton is my salsa instructor and he gave me his number and was pursuing me, up until his girlfriend (who I had no idea about) saw me talking to him at a salsa class. I have never harassed him. I have messages on my phone which prove he was the pursuer. He would call me for thirty minute telephone conversations on multiple occasions. Also, he would grind up against me in salsa lessons, so I could feel his erect, hard penis against me. Is that an appropriate thing for a salsa teacher to be doing?'

'No it's not. I knew there was more to the story as his girlfriend was with him, when he filed the complaint and he seemed fearful of her. Also, he said you were a teacher and he didn't want this to affect your career in any way'.

'Well yeah, considering I haven't done anything wrong and he is making a false accusation, I should think not' I laughed down the phone.

'Well unfortunately as he has made this accusation, we need to send you a warning letter. This will not be an official letter and will not go down on any records, but it is just a letter warning you to keep away from Newton Barnes.

'Ok not a problem', I reply. WOW!!!

Chapter 26 - Gorwood

June, 2023

Last term. Had a break down on the second day in. Monday was training day and Tegan and Michella decided to embarrass me in front of everyone. I know they mean well and in their eyes, it was just fun banter, but for me it was mortifying being brought to the whole room's attention. I like them both, but it's the first time they have made me feel really uncomfortable.

"Maria make me a coffee, Maria I need milk, Maria do this, Maria do that". I'm not witty and can't think of good comebacks until at least two days later, so I made them their drinks, but when they wouldn't stop embarrassing me, I said weakly "Shut up you two, I'm trying to keep a low profile here, I'm trying to blend into the background".

The next day I was covering Year 3 in the morning and Year 1 in the afternoon. The TA Amanda Bedhead kept taking over my class in the morning and then the Year 6 teacher ignored me when I said hello to him. A couple of other teachers were being off with me and I just felt a bit shit overall. Not sure why I let other people affect me, but maybe I was feeling low anyway. I ended up having a breakdown at lunchtime, and went off sick the next day. The doctor has now signed me off for 2 weeks. Although I'm feeling bored now lol. Why is my life such a mess?

Dating is crap but being alone is crap. Dealing with unrequited love is crap! Life is crap!

On the other hand, I have a king sized bed all to myself. I can eat what I want. I have way more orgasms alone anyway as my special toy is way more satisfying than a man has ever been. I can watch films, read books, eat delicious food. I have a lot to be grateful for. I had 3 amazing job offers from 3 schools; all male headteachers. Prior to those offers, I got rejected at 4 schools all with female headteachers. I was worried at the time, but am now so glad they rejected me as these schools were so much better. I had a Year 1 job offer in Ampthill, a KS1 job offer in Leighton Buzzard and a PPA role in Luton. I could easily reject the Ampthill one as it was only a years contract, whereas the other 2 were permanent. PPA is my dream role as less stress, as don't have to deal with all the classroom responsibilities of parents evenings, report writing, displays, progress of children, parents complaining etc. The Leighton Buzzard school was lovely people though (or so it seems).

Had a week off work now and so bored. I've realised that work is important, as all play and no work is almost as boring as all work and no play. I'm going back tomorrow. Crazy as I could have taken the next 6 weeks off if I had wanted, but I wanted to go back. As soon as I went back, I started my period .... Bad timing and then a week later, I had really bad lower back pain. I was in agony and struggled to bend. It hurt when I sneezed, laughed or coughed. I went to the doctors and he signed me off until the end of term. The only good thing about going into work everyday was I got to see Ben and the teachers were lovely. I prayed to God every day that if he would heal me and the pain stopped, that I would never complain again about not having true love. I am now 99 percent healed and know that I will be completely healed very soon. I am so grateful and am going to stick to my promise to God. Thank you God for healing me. I love you and always will. I must keep reminding myself of this every time I crave romantic love in the future.

Chapter 27 – What happens next?

July 2023

I don't know what will happen next or how my journey will develop ... but I'm going to go into it with faith that God is with me and it will turn out for the best. Everything I have ever dreamed of is coming to me. I am grateful for my life, my health, my family, my friends, my job. I know I am blessed to have all these things when not everyone does. Thank you God. Thank you for helping me get three job offers from 3 schools and helping me make the right decision over which school to choose.... I hope. Thank you for helping me earn enough money, so that I can help my parents enjoy the rest of their lives without worrying over finances. Thank you for finding me the perfect house. Thank you for making me earn enough money, so that my mum can be my personal dresser. I am manifesting all of this by stating it before I receive it. Thank you for putting me in a position so that I can help others. Thank you for everything. Thank you for loving me so much and saving me many times in my life. Thank you for all the people who make my life beautiful. I am lucky to have so many wonderful people in my life and I now leave the rest to God. I have deleted all the dating apps. They are not for me. If I'm meant to have a partner to share my life with and who I'm madly in love with, it will happen for me and if I'm meant to remain single for the rest of my life, then I'm ok with that too, as I can't force it. Whatever will be, will be. I am alive and where there is life, there is hope and where there is hope, there is always a chance for dreams to become reality. I am not perfect and have made many mistakes, but I am where I am and know that good things are coming ...... As when you ask for things with a good heart and your intentions are pure, then the whole universe conspires to make your dreams come true! Or so I hoped.

Chapter 28 – Happy ending?

January 1st 2024

Meedon Lower School. I feel protected and safe in this school. Thank you god, for bringing these people into my life. That is enough. More than enough. I hope I am right!

I feel like I am too old for love now anyway, so I am going to relax and leave the rest to you now God. Let's see what happens!

On my death bed, let it be known, there once lived a girl, who never stopped believing in the beauty of her dreams and always followed her heart! Xxx

Chapter 29 – Too good to be true

30th December 2024

Wow!! How much a year can change things. Whatever could happen did happen this year. I thought this was a school I could finally feel safe and happy in. I was on a permanent contract in Year 2. I was offered Wednesdays off to work from home doing my PPA, although later it changed to the PPA being on Friday's so each year group could plan together. The headteacher seemed kind and caring and I actually felt protected by every member of the school. There were nine men in this school and although that was strange for a lower school and I had never worked with so many before, it actually made me feel safer for some reason. The deputy headteacher was also amazing, but from January 2024 to July 2024, something changed. I had a colleague called Sharon Pew who seemed determined to make my life as difficult as possible, who was constantly criticising me, making embarrassing comments in the staffroom towards me, trying to slander my name, talking about sex constantly, gossiping and slagging people off in the staff room, making racist comments and overall making me feel like shit. She often didn't do the planning properly and was constantly lying to my face and to others about me. One day I walked into the staffroom to eat my lunch, as I could hear Sharon slagging off Simon; the caretaker. William Jenson;

the headteacher also came in not long after me to eat his lunch.

'Simon is such a creep. I wouldn't have him near the children. He's a weirdo. Anyway, he loves you Maria, but then you encourage it. You hug him and stuff', Sharon declared in front of the whole staff room. I felt mortified. Did she actually just say that in front of everyone and the headteacher? I didn't encourage Simon. I was nice to him because he was always nice and respectful towards me. Plus I knew how awful it felt to be ignored and left out from my school days and I didn't want anyone else to ever feel like that.

'No I don't. I'm too nice', I replied weakly, not knowing how else to respond in the moment. Feeling embarrassed, I started to put loads of ketchup on my chips, as I love ketchup. Suddenly, Sharon brought the whole room's attention on to me again and all I wanted to do was eat my lunch in peace without being constantly humiliated.

'I didn't know Indians ate ketchup. Are you actually Indian?', asked Sharon Pew, looking at me with mock humour. Why was she bringing my ethnic origin into the conversation and differentiating me from everyone at the table? I wanted to fit in and feel like I belonged, not made to feel that I was different from everyone else. She had made comments like this quite a few times now and I really hated it. Feeling embarrassed again, I just laughed it off.

'Oh I love ketchup. Do you want some?' I asked her.

'No it's fine', she said as she got up to walk out of the staffroom. I quickly ate the rest of my lunch and left to return to my classroom and prepare for my next lesson.

I talked about this incident that weekend with my family and friends. They were shocked.

'Why did you let her get away with saying those things? You should have calmly asked her (at the time) what she meant by the 'encouraging Simon' comment', said my mum. 'You're so naive'.

'I know mum, but you know me. I can never think of what to say on the spot'. The next day I sent a long email to the headteacher about it. I felt I needed to say something, as I had noticed for some time now that the headteachers attitude towards me had changed considerably since Sharon Pew had been spending more time with him and being in his ear. I had a sneaky suspicion that she was saying more things like that to him about me, trying to diminish my value in the headteachers eyes, by gossiping about me and my interactions with the men in the school. It seemed to happen, the more Sharon Pew spread lies and gossip about me and she always seemed to be in his office or trying to do things for him, to keep him on side I'm guessing. This was maybe how she seemed to get away with treating others like shit, who didn't benefit her in anyway. She was a clever cookie alright.

So much has happened, it's difficult to process. I got suspended from work on July 1st 2024. How did this happen? An investigation went on for 6 months and then I was sacked for gross misconduct on the 16th December, 2024 while I was signed off sick by my doctor. I was also informed that this would be referred to the TRA (Teaching regulation agency) for them to consider whether I should be barred from teaching. I didn't react very well to this as in my mind it was a massive injustice. I had been professional and a good teacher all year, until I got pushed out of character on one day. A day I was trying to make a point; that unprofessional behaviour (by Sharon Pew) gets rewarded at Meedon Lower School. My mum and sister supported me at the final disciplinary appeal hearing on Friday 31st January, 2025.

A few days before my misconduct, another incident happened in which the headteacher; Willliam Jenson stuck up for Sharon Pew.   After all she had put me through and my multiple complaints about Sharon, I couldn't understand why he was always protecting her and seemed to be against me.   Martha Dunn called me. 'Hey Maria. So today Sharon was making inappropriate comments about Simon again. When you left your after school club with Simon, I overheard Sharon saying 'I wouldn't leave my class alone with Simon. He's a perv'.

'But I only had three children in the class and they were doing mindful colouring in my after school club at 4pm', I said to Martha. 'I desperately needed the toilet and had one thing to photocopy so I was literally two minutes.'

'I know. You did nothing wrong Maria. Anyway, I went to complain to the headteacher, Mr. Jenson about it and said to him that Sharon shouldn't be making comments like that about the cleaner Simon, as it is destroying a good man's reputation and character, but his response was 'well that's not Sharon's fault, that's Maria's fault', Martha informed me.

'Wow, why is it my fault? I needed the toilet and it was after school hours and was only three children. Also, Willliam has employed Simon as a cleaner, so surely he has been DBS checked and he wouldn't be employing people who are paedophiles', I argued.

'Yeah you're absolutely right, but I defended you and said that it's not Maria's fault. It's Sharon's fault as she shouldn't be making comments like that'.

'I don't understand why William keeps defending Sharon', I exclaimed. 'All she does is make inappropriate comments, talk about sex, how good she is at giving blowjobs, anal sex, escort agencies, only fans etc, she flashes her breasts and bum in team meetings and Christmas parties. Is that the reason he always defends her? Maybe she's offering him something?', I said to Martha.

'Yeah me and my husband thought the same thing. It is strange how he's always defending her, no matter how inappropriate and unprofessional she is. I mean she talks about escort agencies and only fans and he doesn't bat an eyelid,' stated Martha.

'Yeah he was so supportive of me at the start of my time at Meedon, but somehow Sharon has turned him against me. She's definitely got to be giving him something. How dare he say 'it's Maria's fault and not Sharon's, when she is the one slandering a good mans name, by implying Simon is a paedophile. It should be safe to leave three children alone with him for two minutes while I go to the toilet. I mean William is the one that has employed Simon and I'm guessing he wouldn't employ a man who is a danger to children,' I said. Martha and I talked for a little longer, before we said our goodbyes for the night.

This incident, as well as the fact that William Jenson gave Sharon Pew her preference of year group, when he had already agreed with me that I could remain in Year 2, plus everything I had endured at the hands of Sharon Pew over the course of the year, is ultimately what was the catalyst for my misconduct on one day. I honestly felt that at Meedon Lower School, sexually inappropriate behaviour is what gets rewarded. And the professional teachers like me get punished instead, so I stupidly thought that maybe if I act more like Sharon Pew, maybe I will get rewarded with the year group of my choice too and William Jenson might change his mind. But such is life; it is rarely fair and just and nothing ever goes the way we think it will. If I had known the repercussions of my actions on the 27th June 2024, I would have kept quiet or stayed off sick as all my friends and family had advised. Silly stupid me!

Chapter 30

Friday 31st January, 2025

Disciplinary Appeal Hearing

I woke up at 7am and got a taxi to the gym. My sister Sarita picked me up and we drove to my mums to get ready for the hearing. The night before I had just found out that my ex, Steve Peck had died from bile duct cancer. I had not slept much all night. I had seen a facebook status on his best friends profile, saying how he had 'lost the best friend a man could ask for.' I was in shock. It couldn't be. I messaged his friend who confirmed that Steve had been diagnosed with terminal cancer in May 2024. This was around the same time Steve had asked me not to contact him ever again. Now it all made sense. We had been back in contact in March and had gone cinema together to watch the film 'Dune 2' and we were talking about going on a holiday together in August and meeting up again to play darts and poole. I had loved him once. I realised I still loved him but it was too late now. He was gone. I found out from his friend Phil, that Steve had loads of chemo and treatments after he had been diagnosed and then he ended up having a blood clot in his foot in December. They had to amputate his left leg! Oh my god! How awful for him. Then he had died anyway on January 29th 2025. I found out the night before my hearing.

At the hearing, there were a panel of 8 people, only two I recognised, Heather Trudge who was the investigating officer and Elouise Harrison; the office manager for the school. They all introduced themselves and me and my sister introduced ourselves. My sister started with the disclaimer of the fact that my ex had died from cancer. Then Emily Holden gave a brief chat of why I was there and the fact that I had made sexual remarks to the headteacher on one day on the 27th June and sent a sexual message to him. I was then allowed to present my defence to the panel, which I then read out to them.

My Disciplinary Statement

I would like to open with a scenario. I want you all to imagine that you are a teacher with a class of 30 children. And in that class you have 2 children who stand out. One child (let's call her Sherrie) she's constantly rude and disrespectful, she swears, she talks about inappropriate things on a daily basis, she flashes her private parts to other children and so on. Then there's another child (let's call her Megan) and she's polite and respectful to everyone, she's kind to everyone including the cleaner because she's been taught by her parents to treat others the way she would want to be treated. She never swears, she never talks about inappropriate things and she's a high performer. She always completes her work to a high standard and is generally always well behaved and considerate. You've taught both these children for nearly a year, so you know both their characters quite well. As a teacher, if you overhear Sherrie saying something rude and disrespectful or talking about sex, you don't think anything of it, as it's a normal daily occurrence, but if suddenly Megan starts acting out of character and talking about sex and saying things that seem disrespectful, you're sitting there thinking 'What's going on? That's not normal. What's happened to Megan? What could be the underlying cause that pushed her to act out so completely out of character? As a teacher, would you be concerned and try to find out what's going on or would your immediate reaction be one of judgement and expulsion? Adults are no different from children in that we are just as sensitive to bullying, slander, gossip and constant criticism and being led to suicidal feelings because of the environment we are in. I would like to read out a face book post that I presented as evidence, which talks about my feelings on this.

'I'm watching 13 reasons why and it really hits home how one false rumour can ruin or destroy

someone's life! Kid's can be just as cruel as adults. Having been on the receiving end of this myself at school, I know how it can make you feel completely alone. It is so important to teach our kids to be kind, honest and treat others the way they would want to be treated!'

This post is dated June 2020, so was 5 years ago. I would ask all of you sitting on this panel today, to bear this scenario and post in mind as I go through my statement today. I would also like to point out that I never made any sexual moves on William Jenson before that day or after that day. This is about my misconduct on one day and one day alone. And was a mistake I immediately apologised for and many times since. All of the evidence I have presented overwhelmingly proves that I am actually the complete opposite of that type of woman you hear in that text message.

I would like to start by saying that my parents have always taught me to be more concerned about my character than my reputation, as my character is who I actually am, but my reputation is simply what is said about me. I can honestly sit in front of you all today and look you in the eye and say I am so proud of who I am. I have always lived my life with high moral standards, integrity and compassion. Am I proud of that text message I sent William Jenson on the 27th June? 100 percent not. While I deeply regret that message, (and please note I showed remorse as soon as I sent it), I want to make it clear that is not who I am or ever has been or ever will be. Am I proud of who I am as a person and my true character? One million percent yes. I take full responsibility for my actions that day and have done since the very start of this investigation, but I ask that you consider the mitigating factors and evidence I provide.

William Jenson deep down knows I am a good person as do all the witnesses who I named on my grievance form, many of whom were never questioned about my grievances, which directly relate to my misconduct on the 27th June and I have evidence they were never questioned about the racism and inappropriate sexual comments made by Sharon Pew on a daily basis. I have received proof they were never questioned about these parts of my grievances in messages I have received directly from them. This leaves a massive gap in the investigation. Jo Shellon (who is the vice president of governors at Meedon) actually said at the end of my grievance appeal 'Maria no one is questioning your character'. I thanked her for this at the time in an email and told her I really appreciated the fact that she could see the truth of my good character. And I will say it again, I am someone of good morals and character. William Jenson knows that throughout the year I always treated him and every member of staff at Meedon Lower School with nothing but respect and kindness and if you look at all the evidence, you can clearly see that any correspondence I had with William Jenson actually shows me showing him a huge amount of respect, apart from on that one day on the 27th June. It is important to address the portrayal of me in Heather Trudge's report. I have read Heather Trudge's report on me in full and I can honestly say her portrayal of me as a person is 1000 percent false and today I will be disputing every single point in her report, using my evidence to do so. I know that most of you will already have made up your mind and don't care what I say today, but despite knowing this, and knowing you are all my goliath, I am going to speak my truth and I will never stop speaking my truth until the day I die. Heather Trudge has claimed I have no evidence. This is completely untrue and today I will be reading out some of this evidence to back up all my points and prove that Heather Trudge has covered up the truth and demonised me in order to avoid the school being held accountable for any wrongdoing. In court, I will happily take a lie detector test for any evidence I don't have. Apart from that message, there is no actual evidence for anything else that has been said about me, apart from what I already owned up to. This is because I am genuinely a good, decent person and everyone that knows me knows that, including William Jenson. I have extensive evidence of my suffering and that I have spoken the truth throughout this investigation. I also have evidence of the lies spoken by others. Heather Trudge has truly done a great job of covering up the truth and painting me as a villain. If the school wants to make a good person a villain to escape any accountability, so be it, but I will never stop speaking my truth.

Heather Trudge's characterisation of me in her report as 'angry' is inaccurate. I am not an angry person. All my family, friends and many colleagues would vouch for the fact that I value peace and harmony and strive to avoid conflict. I actually spoke several times to William Jenson over the course of the year, telling him that I don't like conflict and I like peace and harmony. He responded 'yes. I know you've said that several times' back in June. I am only angry when severely provoked and as I said to William and Rick (the head of year and my direct line manager) back in September 2023, only 3 things make me angry;

injustice, unfairness and hypocrisy. My emotional state during the June meeting with Heather and Jane stemmed from the overwhelming stress I had endured throughout the year. This stress significantly impacted my mental health and I made my struggles known to various colleagues. I was also honest about feeling on the verge of a breakdown in a phone call I had with William Jenson on the 17th June. My doctors note also corroborates this, but unfortunately this has not been acknowledged in the report. As I had been upset and crying during that meeting and told her I wanted to die, Heather seemed to show a lot of concern at the time for my emotional mental state and her and Jane asked me if I would like to talk to anyone in the school and I said Abraham Raft (who is the deputy headteacher).

I always strived to have a professional relationship with every member of staff in the school and my relationship with every man in the school was always a professional one. This is why I was so upset when Sheryl Pew tried to slander my name in the staff room earlier this year and I would like to read the email I sent to William, Abrahim and Rick following this meeting.

Hi William, (CC Abrahim, Rick),

I wasn't very happy with a comment Sharon made at lunchtime about Simon being in love with me and that I encourage him and cuddle him as that is a complete lie!!!

I have never cuddled Simon or encouraged him in any way. I am pleasant and nice to him like I am nice to everyone. I didn't say much I response at the time, as I can't always think on the spot what to say, plus I didn't want to make a scene in front of everyone. However, I feel that she keeps making sly comments like that to put shade on my character. I have a professional relationship with EVERY man in this school and although I didn't say anything this time, next time she makes comments about my character even as a joke (which are complete lies), I will erupt and call her out to her face in front of everyone. I am just telling you that now.

I respect you as a leader and headteacher and really hope you understand my point of view. You don't need to say or do anything about it right now. I will deal with it myself next time it happens.

Maria

This email was sent on the 8th June, only a few weeks before I behaved out of character on the 27th June. You can clearly see that I am showing William Jenson respect in this email as you will see in all my correspondence with him throughout the year. This shows the truth of my character and the fact that I felt so offended by Sharon Pew's comments in the staffroom. I know the school wants to pick on the word 'erupt', but I was simply expressing how insulted I felt by what had been said, as this was nothing new with Sharon Pew. And this is also because I am a woman of high morals and ethics, as opposed to Sharon Pew who clearly had none and proudly talked about how she had no regrets about the multiple affairs she has had with married men. I am a woman who would never sleep with a man I am not in love with. That is 100 percent the truth and cannot be changed because of one text message which does NOT reflect who I am. I have provided evidence to the school of the truth of my character and if you had all viewed this, you would know that.

Heather Trudge also states in her report about me being in competition with Sharon Pew. There is no competition as my planning far exceeded hers in both quality and the fact that is was actually done. This is not me bragging but the actual truth. In Sharon Pew's statement to Andrea Bennings, she claimed that the reason she was constantly coming to criticise me and tell me what to do, was because she was the more experienced teacher. Yet William Jenson claimed in his report to Heather Trudge that the reason he was moving me to Year 3 was because he felt I was the more experienced teacher. So who was lying? Sharon or William?? ... Sharon was lying as she always did throughout my experience with her. I was the more experienced and better teacher and this fact annoyed Sharon and made her feel insecure and jealous and that was the reason she was constantly belittling me. She knew I was the better woman in both work ethic and character. This was also why she told Simon Linch that I was a 'princess', implying that I was a goody two shoes. I was. This was why she felt it necessary to continually put me down, as many colleagues at Meedon often pointed out to me and told me not to let her get to me. They told me 'it's her insecurity Maria. She knows you're a woman of good morals and character, whereas she has none.' Stacey Walliams also expressed to me how shocked she is that someone like Sharon who was constantly talking about sex is doing working in a school. Martha who covered my class on Wednesdays confirmed in her witness statement that my planning was always there and was also done to a really high standard, but Sharon Pew's was not. In contrast to the many lies in Rick Enning's (my year lead) statement which I will be using actual evidence to corroborate later. Abraham Raft also confirmed this in his witness statement. Rick was constantly praising me throughout the year for my 'brilliant power points and worksheets'' as he put it. He never once criticised me about anything. In fact he would go above and beyond to help me, often staying back late to help me. Heather Trudge states that the school has no knowledge of me being on the 'verge of a breakdown' or of my mental wellbeing. This is a complete and utter lie. I told William Jenson, when he called me on my first day of sickness on the 17th June, that I was on the verge of a breakdown. This was also the day that he chose to inform me that I would be moved out of year 2, something that had already been agreed before the resignation date. If the school would like to call my doctor, I am happy for them to corroborate this, but I also have a doctors note which I presented as evidence and would like to read out now. I would like to remind you that this was only 10 days or so before I committed my misconduct on the 27th June.

To whom it may concern,

Miss. Maria Bassett is registered at Putnoe Medical centre. I can confirm that Miss. Bassett had a consultation on the 14th of June 2024. The consultation was about stress related to her work environment. She has reported suicidal thoughts, however there was no active plans. She was advised to self-certify for 7 days of sick leave.

Yours sincerely,

**Doctor Bhaskar*

The doctor now regrets not signing me off for longer. Heather Trudge talks about my social phobia and how I have no official diagnosis, but as well as all my family, I spoke to several colleagues about this over the year, including Abrahim Raft (the deputy headteacher) and Martha who actually mentions this when she was questioned over Teams and in her character reference.

Heather Trudge concludes her report her of me, by stating that my behaviour on the 27th June was planned and premeditated over ten days. This is a completely false portrayal of what happened and who I am as a person. There is nothing conniving or premeditated about me. Everyone that knows me, including many of my colleagues at Meedon would actually describe me as innocent and kind. Yes I had asked William to reconsider his decision and stated my reasons why, including the fact that we had a verbal agreement before the resignation date. I had then resigned when he declined and this email also shows me showing William Jenson respect. He did not want me to resign and this email is dated 21st June, 2024. So only six days before my misconduct,

William Jenson was still eager for me to remain in the school. Why is this if I am such a bad teacher? This is because he knows I was a good teacher and good person with a good heart. Everyone knows that I do not have an agenda of any kind. All I want is peace and harmony, for myself and for others. I will read the email I sent to William Jenson after he had told me to reconsider my resignation.

To: William Jenson, (CC Abrahim Raft; Rick Enning)

Thank you William. I won't be changing my mind on this, as I don't want to teach Year 3 and may even leave teaching altogether. I want a chance to have a life outside of teaching and if I can't remain in Year 2 and consolidate what I have already spent the year doing the hard work for, then I am happy to hand you my resignation next Thursday in writing.

Thank you for everything and I hope we can leave on good terms, as regardless of what you think, I do have huge respect for you aa a headteacher and a human being. You are free to make your choices and if you feel that you have made the right ones and can't change your mind from that, then I respect and accept that.

Maria

Again this email shows me showing William Jenson nothing but respect as I showed him throughout my time at Meedon Lower School. Please note this was sent only six days before my misconduct and he did not want me to resign. I also copied in Abrahim into this email.

Heather Trudge talks about how she believes there is no causal link between what I have endured and my actions on the 27th June. This is a complete and utter lie. My parents are here today listening to all of this and they have seen the message I sent William and they know that it could not be the furthest thing from my true character possible. I wanted them to be here today to hear everything and all the mud that is being thrown at my name. My parents and everyone that knows me are constantly telling me; Maria you are such a hermit, all you do is stay home and watch Netflix. You need to get out more. I literally go to work, go swimming and then come home and watch films or do planning. Rick Enning was in Year 2 for over eight years, but there still seemed to be a lot of planning for us all to do, so I'm not sure why Heather Trudge is saying the planning is already done. In my head, it was going to be starting all over again in year 3. Why do you all think that 40,000 teachers quit the profession last year and the average a teacher stays in the profession when they first qualify is 3 years before they crumble under the pressure and leave the career? This is because there is no work life balance. However, remaining in the same year group where you can reuse and tweak your previous planning massively reduces this stress. The reason there's such a massive teacher shortage is directly because of the excessive workload. Even Rick Enning stated to me several times that he wished he could find something else.

Heather Trudge has said in her report how I sent an angry email after I got suspended to Nicole. This is completely untrue and false. I would like to read out that email to you all now, dated 2nd July 2024.

Thank you Nicole. Yes I am happy to do that and will send you that soon. Whatever decision is made I will accept it, as things that have happened over the course of this year have mentally and physically drained me.

I would like to say at this time that I feel ashamed and embarrassed that I allowed my anger and frustration at the continuous injustice that has happened to me over this year get the better of me. I should never have sent that message to William and I regretted it as soon as I sent it and have regretted it every day since. Anyone that

knows me, knows that is not who I am as person and never has been.

The truth is as someone who was betrayed by someone she loved at 22, I've never even had an orgasm with a man. My first experience was bad, and apart from 2 short relationships, I generally keep away from men and would NEVER send ANY man a message like that, let alone my boss!!! I felt like that was the only way I could get my point across; that people who break all the rules seem to get rewarded in this school and people who follow every rule, (as I did up until last week) get punished! As I said yesterday, Sharon has consistently talked about sex nearly every day since being at this school; anal sex, how good she is at blowjobs, how horny she is, she's dying for it, how nice William smells, she has flashed her bum in team meetings, emulated sex etc etc. She then tried to slander my reputation, by making comments about me and the cleaner, Simon (who I have been nothing but kind and respectful too) and constantly slanders him off too. She also slags people off in the staff room. Instead of any consequence (just a code of conduct) she was then rewarded with the year group of her choice and 22 children. I on the other hand followed EVERY rule and then got told I have to start again from scratch in a new year group, and move classes again, which I was not expecting, as

William had assured me I could stay in year 2 before the resignation date, which was why I decided to stay.

In the first term at Meedon, I had a really good relationship with William and every member of staff and apart from Sharon, I still do. William was supportive and kind to me. One day when Charlie was being a nightmare, he put him in Sharon's class the next day to "give Miss Bassett a break" as he said. I really appreciated that. When I revealed to him I suffered with social phobia and didn't like being directly addressed in staff meetings, he made sure I never was again and would often come and sit next to me, to make sure I felt safe and comfortable. I really appreciated that and it's the first school, I felt really protected by all the men. I've never felt safe being around or talking to men in schools before and as it's usually women in schools, this has never been a problem. But I remember feeling totally safe around William and every man at the start and this may have led to me thinking I had a slight crush. But over the year, as Sharon has eroded my confidence with her false accusations, and has been able to get away with it, I stopped feeling safe or feeling anything for anyone. All I wanted to do was get on with my job to the best of my ability and I am sure Rick would validate (although he didn't) that I have done a much better job at this than Sharon has over the year and I was really looking forward to reaping the benefits of this in September by consolidating. I had just got used to the fact that I would be in year 3, when I found out that there would actually be 3 classes in year 2 and Sharon and Rick would only have 22 children each! This was a further blow to me. I should have probably let it go, but in my anger and frustration, I could not fathom how Sharon had got so lucky after everything she has put me through this year, constantly coming into my classroom and criticising me, when my planning is far better than hers and anyone can tell you in the school I am very organised!

I would like to end up by saying that I can't apologise to William enough for the message I sent him which was a complete mistake (the one mistake I've made, when Sharon has made hundreds over the year) and I will send you the list shortly of all she has put me through. I admire and respect William and always have and the fact is that before Sharon started spreading false rumours about me, he had shown me nothing but kindness and compassion as a teacher and a human being. I am really sad that it has got to this stage and that everyone in this school and people I think highly of will think badly of me because of one mistake I have made in a moment of anger!

This whole situation has made me suicidal and every day I am kept away from school and people at school are left to think I am the worst person in the world, when I know I am not is slowly killing me on the inside, but I know I have to be strong for my dad who has been on the verge of a heart attack and my mum and whole family. As I need to be their strength, I cannot talk to them about it. I just have my friends. Anyway, I will send you the list as soon as I've put it together about Sharon, but if you all still want me to leave after that it is fine, I will accept it.

Kind regards,
Maria Bassett

As you can see, that is by no means an angry message as Heather Trudge has falsely claimed in her report. It was actually an honest and heartfelt message with me again apologising and explaining my behaviour that day. Since that email, I provided evidence which proves that I was speaking the truth and is also evidence of the truth of my character. Heather Trudge goes onto say that the mitigation I have provided does not explain my behaviour on the 27th June. I would argue that is completely false and untrue. First of all, my evidence proves beyond all doubt that it was out of character. Please look at the message I sent Rick Enning when he was messaging me at 11pm at night on the 17th November 2023. We're talking about how I hate dating and he says;

'Yeah dating is hard. Too much disappointment and awkwardness.'

I respond 'Yeah plus I love my own company. It's the best. If I'm not madly in love, it's not worth it. Never was and never will be.'

Rick Enning responds with a blushing face emoji and then texts 'You got that chess app yet?'

I acted totally out of character on the 27th June last year and that is a mitigating factor. The other mitigating factor is my poor mental health and the fact I have a doctors note which proves this only 10 days before my misconduct. Both Stacey Walliams and Martha Dunn also sent me emails urging me to join a trade union due to what I had endured over the year. My poor mental health was due to work related stress and this was directly caused by the bullying, harassment, slander and racism I endured at the hands of Sharon Pew. I would now like to refer you to Martha Dunn's witness statement which talks not only about the extensive bullying, harassment and constant criticism I endured at the hands of Sharon Pew but also the sexual harassment I endured at her hands. She mentions the sexual talk in some detail and I would like to read out the just the last two paragraphs in her lengthy witness statement to you all now.

At the beginning of the school year Maria would spend time in the staff room but after all the

'derogatory' comments and the sexual talk Maria withdrew herself from the staffroom and eating on her own in her classroom. She became withdrawn and began experiencing headaches and at times vomiting with stress. These were all from January onwards and were physical signs of stress. I often went into Maria's room to sit with her as she was withdrawn and isolated.

The general sexual talk was quite prolific and I did, when I heard something that crossed the boundaries raise it with SLT. I didn't hear anything about Maria but I have heard inappropriate comments from Sharon about other members of staff. I can share, however they don't relate to Maria.

As you can clearly hear from this statement, my mental health was severely affected by all I had endured at the hands of Sharon Pew. Martha and every member of staff in the school knows that I was a woman who would never talk about sex. The fact that I had to listen to this every day in the staff room is a form of sexual harassment. The fact that it caused me to withdraw into my classroom and made me feel sick is also a form of abuse. If all the employees at Meedon Lower School had been questioned about this, you would have quickly realised the extent of the problem. As I am woman who actually has strong morals and ethics and have never been involved with someone I don't have feelings for, I found this difficult to deal with. You definitely should not be constantly talking about sex in a school working with children, but that is who Sharon Pew is. I am the complete opposite of that and anyone who knows me knows that. So this now covers the mitigating factors that it was completely out of character and I experienced much personal trauma through bullying, harassment, slander, racism and sexual harassment by Sharon Pew, which severely affected my mental health. Abraham Raft confirmed the racist comments by Sharon Pew, where she said I was 'indianising things' and she also said 'I didn't know Indian people ate ketchup. Are you actually indian?' and this was said in the staff room in front of multiple witnesses but has never been investigated and most schools would take this very seriously. I was mortified by all these comments as it separated me from everyone else and made me feel like I am not the same as everyone else by pointing out my race in a conversation in public. As Abraham Raft (the deputy headteacher at Meedon) said to me in June, 'Maria this place has hurt you. It's better for you to leave.' Despite raising my concerns about Sharon Pew's behaviour, no formal action was taken against her, and her breaches of the code of conduct were ignored. Meanwhile, my one mistake has led to my suspension and dismissal. This disparity in treatment is unjust and has compounded my sense of frustration and betrayal by the school.

The other mitigating factor is my previous impeccable track record. Abrahim Raft confirmed the fact that I was a dedicated teacher. I was often the first in and last to leave. I always had my planning done and it was always completed to an exceptional standard as Rick Enning was constantly telling me this throughout the year. Rick would often come and complain to me about Sharon Pew and would often say 'I've had enough of this. I need to go and speak to William about Sharon'. Martha Dunn and Abrahim Raft also confirmed that when they had to cover my class, they never had a problem with anything I had prepared. It was Sharon Pew's planning they had a problem with, not just the lack of it, but also the quality.

All of the mitigating factors are there and Heather Trudge is giving a completely false portrayal of me to cover up for the school and let them get away with everything I have endured over the year. This is completely unjust and unfair. I am a kind, decent, loving person with a good character and good morals and everyone that knows me knows that. You cannot change my true character based on one text message I immediately apologised for and was sent on the edge of a mental breakdown and suicidal thoughts.

And that is all the hard evidence the school has; one text message and the fact that I didn't lie and had the decency and integrity to own up to my mistake from the start of the investigation, but others have decided to lie instead. I have a huge amount of evidence which proves all my suffering and if you look at all the evidence, you will know I am speaking the truth. If this goes to the tribunal and is referred to the Teaching regulation agency, (as well as making my own referrals for sexual harassment and racism), I would also question why Sharon Pew was allowed to get away with so much.

Heather Trudge claims in her report that I don't have any evidence of a verbal agreement between William and I, but I have direct text messages between William and I that prove there was a verbal agreement as well as an email I sent colleagues. I would like to point out that a verbal agreement is binding by law and it doesn't have to be in a contract.

The week prior to the incident that occurred on the 27th June, I had been advised by my doctor to self certify for 7 days, due to stress related to my work environment and having had suicidal thoughts. I made the mistake of coming back early, having found out during a phone call from my headteacher, William Jenson on my first day of sickness on Monday 17th June, that I would be moved to Year 3 in September. I was very surprised by this as William had made a verbal agreement with me before the resignation date that I could remain in Year 2 in September and this helped me make the decision not to resign. I have provided text evidence to the school which supports this. The fact that this had then changed after the resignation date and during my sick leave further impacted my mental health. The only reason I resigned was because William Jenson had breached this verbal agreement.

I would like it to be noted at this point that during my meeting with Heather, I was informed that William denied all knowledge of me telling him that I was on the verge of a breakdown. However, this was the truth as my doctors note I sent to the school now proves. I said breakdown as I didn't want to say suicidal thoughts over the phone, so I said breakdown which my doctor said she would be happy to corroborate in court if it ever needed to go that far. William later changed his strong denial of a verbal agreement to then saying in his statement that he never promised me Year 2, but as far as I am concerned a verbal agreement is a verbal agreement and binding by law. Also, the fact that he is even saying he never promised anything, implies that there was an agreement to begin with. When I asked him if I could remain in Year 2 before the resignation date, he clearly said and I quote 'yeah if that's where you want to be that's fine'. If you look at the text messages between William and I, he doesn't once deny it and he could have denied it, if that was the truth. I would like to read out these text messages.

'Hello Maria. Just called and left you a message for you to call regarding illness and next year. If you can give me a call please when you are able. Thanks William.'

'Tried to call you back William. Does that mean I will be going up with my own class to Year 3 or one of the other Year 2's?' I respond.

'No, not yours.'

'Was there a reason I couldn't stay in Year 2 as wanted to consolidate?'

'Hello. I'm happy to explain the reasons why when you return to school next week. Try and get some rest and don't worry about school. Thanks William.'

'Only it's because you had said before half term I could stay in Year 2 if I wanted and it helped me make my decision about whether to resign or not, but I know Sharon really wanted Year 2 as well, but I didn't think her choice would take precedence

over mine, so she will be really happy and feel like she's won. But yeah I'll try and forget about it now. See you next week'.

'Hello I appreciate you are disappointed with my decision but as I said we can discuss this when you return. Thank you.'

As you can hear, when I ask William why he has changed his verbal agreement, he responds with and I quote 'Hello I appreciate you are disappointed with my decision but as I said we can discuss this when you return'. This is because William Jenson 100 percent knows that there was a verbal agreement between us before the resignation date. He doesn't once say that I 'never promised you that' or 'I never said that'. He acknowledges the verbal agreement by responding with 'Hello I appreciate you are disappointed with my decision'. Even Jo Shelldon did acknowledge that this was important evidence at my meeting with her in July, so I'm not sure why this has now changed, apart from the fact that the school doesn't want to accept any liability, but I have already said many times throughout this process that even though I have suffered incredibly at Meedon, I will not pursue this to a tribunal or claim any compensation for my immense suffering as long as I am given a fair outcome. Yet the school still seems to be determined to destroy my life, when I have a huge amount of evidence which proves how much I have suffered; in terms of doctors letters and messages and emails and witness statements, which for some reason Heather Trudge has decided to completely ignore in her report. So rather than apologising to me for my suffering, the school would like to destroy my life instead. I apologised many times for my mistake and yet William Jenson and the school has never issued an apology to me and I know that I deserve one and that many of my colleagues at Meedon would also agree that I deserve one for all I have endured. I am a good person who made one mistake on one day and acted out of character and on the verge of a breakdown as my doctors note proves.

On the day that I made the gross misconduct, I had vomited in my class in front of the whole class and Lorraine Malton (who is a teaching assistant at the school). This was after speaking to William about why I had been moved to a different year group after it had been verbally agreed. I admit I made mistakes in my approach, but after having spent the whole year making complaints about another colleague (and not having it formally dealt with), I was at breaking point. If I had known earlier, the correct procedure for making a formal complaint, I would have done it a lot sooner and we would not be sitting here today, but I am also the type of person that likes to give people the benefit of doubt and multiple chances. I had already been suffering all year due to stress related to my work environment and one colleague in particular. I am very disappointed that those at the top of the school have taken no accountability for any mistakes they have made over the year and instead have decided to twist the truth. The final report does not reflect the truth and Heather, William and Rick are all well aware of this. In his statement, William mentions feeling traumatised by what I said to him in the office, but later after I had vomited in class and had to leave school, William smiled warmly at me as I left school and said 'Hope you feel better soon'. I replied 'Thank you', so that really doesn't make any sense as he was fine with me at that point. William knows he did not suffer any trauma from anything I said to him in person, as I said he smiled warmly at me as I left school.

The reason I was being moved to another Year group was because Sharon Pew and I had to be split up, but I was not expecting that to be me, considering that I was the one who had actually followed all the rules and Sharon Pew was the one who had broken multiple rules in the code of conduct over the course of the year. She has made inappropriate sexual comments throughout the year in front of numerous colleagues, including the headteacher. For example, talking about Only Fans, Escort agencies, anal sex, blow jobs, flirting with the headteacher, talking about having had multiple affairs with staff members. She also flashed her breasts at the staff Christmas party and this had to be stopped by Martha Dunn. She has also flashed her bare bottom during year group meetings. This was all in front of multiple witnesses that the school have refused to question. If you look at the evidence, two of my witnesses have already confirmed this, but this only came out as part of the other investigation on the bullying and slander. To me, these are not professional comments that you should be making in a school where you are working with children and if I was a parent I certainly would not want my child being taught by someone who makes comments like that on a daily basis. (*I now have proof that this has never been investigated, as many of my multiple witnesses have now sent me direct text messages that they were never questioned about this.*) Furthermore, Sharon Pew has made racially offensive comments towards myself, she has slandered my name and others in front of multiple witnesses and on top of all that she would frequently enter my classroom to criticise, bully and harass me about minor things. I found this strange considering I would always have my planning done and there were times she had done nothing. Martha Dunn confirmed all this in her witness statement and she also confirmed that my planning was done to an excellent standard as opposed to Sharon Pew's. Abrahim Raft (the deputy headteacher) also called her a bully and told me not to let her win. Stacey Walliams confirmed that Sharon Pew slandered my name in the staff room and would often take things too far. She also confirmed the prolific sexual talk by Sharon Pew in the staff room. She also lied to me on multiple occasions and I did warn the headteacher back in February of this year, that I was working with someone who kept lying and I did not trust. All of this behaviour was repeated throughout the year, not only towards myself but also other colleagues and even after multiple complaints, no formal action was ever taken. All these things took a massive toll on me and led me to feeling suicidal and to where I am today, sitting in front of you all. This is again where the mitigating factor of my poor mental health comes in due to what I had endured at the hands of Sharon Pew. I was advised by colleagues on a number of occasions during the course of the year to join a union, when I told them of all the challenges I was facing, particularly with this one colleague. I have provided evidence to the school of this. I now understand that they knew where this was heading and they wanted me to have the support behind me. I truly wish I had listened.

When I sent an email to William Jenson back in June, making a complaint about Sharon about her trying to slander my name and humiliate me in the staff room in front of my colleagues, we were both handed a code of conduct the following Monday. On reading the code of conduct, I knew I had not broken any rules in the code of conduct, but Sharon had broken numerous rules and continued to break them even after being handed the code of conduct. William's reasoning for handing it to both of us was apparently in the name of fairness and also because people had heard us shouting in the corridor, but I never left my classroom. I had spoken to Carrie earlier that morning about what had happened the previous Friday and she had told me to just be calm and professional and only speak to her if necessary. I took this advice and stayed in my classroom. Sharon then started to shout at me to come out of my class and talk to her and Alice in the corridor. I said I was busy, but five minutes later she then came into my class and started talking to me and insisting on a hug. When I politely refused, this then resulted in an argument and she started to shout and swear saying she is going to speak to William. I did not understand why I was being handed a code of conduct when I had done nothing wrong.

At this point, I would like to refer to the Meedon code of conduct, which I have read thoroughly. I would say that Sharon Pew consistently breached many of these rules over the course of the year. It states on page 3 that staff should set an example for pupils by 'never using inappropriate or offensive language in school'. Sharon Pew has consistently sworn and made inappropriate sexual comments in the staff room. It also states on page 3 that staff should show 'tolerance and respect for the rights of others and those with different faiths and beliefs'. Sharon Pew has made racist remarks to me and also told Martha Dunn that RE was not an important subject to teach children. It further states in the code of conduct that staff should maintain high standards of honesty and integrity in their role. Yet Sharon Pew consistently lied to my face throughout the year and lied to others about me and has continued to lie during a formal investigation. She was also rude and disrespectful to myself and others throughout the year. The policy also states that staff will not act in a way that brings the school or the teaching profession into disrepute. This also covers sexual misconduct. Sharon Pew went to flash her breasts at the Christmas party and this had to be stopped by Martha Dunn. She has openly talked about escort agencies and ONLY FANS in the staff room and during staff briefings and talked about sex on a daily basis, including anal sex and how much she loves giving blow jobs and how she has no regrets about the multiple affairs she has had with married men. I talked about sex on one day to make a point, (which I apologised for immediately) thinking that this is what gets you rewarded in this school. I followed ALL the rules and was ALWAYS professional and then got punished by being moved out of Year 2 when it had already been agreed I could stay in Year 2. Yet Sharon Pew has had no severe consequences for talking about sex all year and I have been suspended instead. Do you see how this feels very hypocritical and unfair to me? My character has been brought into question, when I was simply trying to make a point while on the edge of a breakdown. I have provided evidence of the truth of my character, so please view this. If Sharon Pew is the role model for the children of Meedon Lower

School, then I truly worry about what the world is coming to.

So my questions to you all today are these; why after breaking so many rules in the code of conduct, as well as the bullying I endured at her hands, why has she still not been suspended? Why has she faced no severe consequences for any of her wrong doing over the course of the year? Why am I the only one that is suspended and now sacked, when others were able to break so many rules in the code of conduct and get away with it? Why am I the only one suffering when the only reason I committed my misconduct was to make a point and see what reward I would get for talking about sex on one day when Sharon Pew had talked about it daily. I was on the verge of a breakdown and having suicidal thoughts (as my doctors note proves) because of all I had endured at the hands of Sharon Pew.

I would again like to stress that my motive for committing the gross misconduct was not a sexual one. I am not and have never been a sexual predator, as Heather Trudge is clearly trying to label me in her report. This investigation that has been started by William is only happening because of everything I have endured in the second investigation that I had started against Sharon Pew. The point I was trying to make was that one employee in the school can break multiple rules in the code of conduct with no real consequences, while another employee who has actually followed all the rules and was already feeling suicidal and at breaking point has gotten punished for breaking one rule on one day. After breaking so many rules, instead of getting punished, Sharon Pew actually got rewarded by getting the year group of her choice with 22 children for the next academic year. I on the other hand who had followed all the rules got punished by being moved out of year 2 and having to start again and learn a whole new curriculum in Key stage 2, when it was actually me and Rick who had done most of the work. In addition, another important point to note is that the week before the incident of misconduct by me, I had actually emailed my resignation to William on the 20th June, having felt very strongly about the injustice and unfairness of being moved out of year 2, when William had already given me his verbal agreement before the resignation date. However, William did not accept my email resignation and wanted it in writing the following week as he wanted to give me time to think about it. The following week, on the morning of Thursday 27th

June (the day of misconduct be me) I discovered that there would actually be 3 classes in Year 2 and I could have actually stayed to consolidate the year, but for some reason William made the decision to let the bully have her preference of year group and consolidate in Year 2, which anyone in the teaching world knows is huge thing. Sharon had often not done any planning throughout the year and there were often arguments between Rick and Sharon about this, which I would have to mediate for. Rick knows that my planning was always done on time and to an excellent standard. I am very disappointed that he decided to say something different during a formal investigation. The injustice of all I have endured over the year is what caused me to act totally out of character. I stupidly thought that acting more like Sharon Pew would prove a point; that unprofessional behaviour gets rewarded in this school. As nothing else had worked. After my mistake on the 27th June, I left my written resignation on William's desk and then vomited soon after in class, due to the stress of the whole situation.

This now brings me to my next point of Rick Enning's many lies in his statement. During a formal investigation on the 15th July this year, Rick Enning criticised my planning and work over the year, saying that the quality of my work was not as good as Sharon Pew's. He said that 'Sharon Pew does things well, but Maria Bassett will just get it done'. He knows this is a complete and utter lie. He always told me my power points were excellent throughout the year. My evidence that I have presented since his statement, shows this. Rick Enning would actually often criticise Sharon Pew's work, as it wasn't only the fact that it often wasn't done, it was also the fact that her work was produced to a really poor standard. Often we were all left with either no planning or half completed planning and worksheets with no date or Learning objective on. Martha Dunn and Abraham Raft have also confirmed this in their statements. Rick also lied when he said in his statement I say 'outlandish things'. This is in complete contradiction to him saying that I was the introvert and Sharon Pew was the extrovert. Rick knows that it was actually Sharon Pew (the extrovert) that was constantly saying outlandish things, NOT me. Rick knows I got on with my work and kept myself to myself as this is what introverts tend to do. Rick was also not telling the full truth, when he said he was often the mediator between Sharon Pew and I. The truth is I was also often the mediator between Rick Enning and Sharon Pew, as they are both strong personalities and would often clash and argue about Sharon Pew's lack of planning. Rick lied again in his statement when he said that 'I don't take things on board or store things long term'. My evidence shows that I would change anything Rick asked me to change. He was constantly thanking me for all I was doing and praising me for my excellent work. There was no point over the year, where he came to speak to me or told me that he wasn't happy with the quality of my work or spoke to me about not having acted on his feedback. He always told me what a great job I was doing, yet his statement says something completely different. Rick Enning lied again when he said that both Sharon Pew and I are on permanent contracts. I was on a permanent contract. My understanding was that Sharon Pew was on a fixed term contract as back around March time, she had been overheard (by Martha Dunn I think) asking William Jenson if she could stay on in September. William had apparently responded 'he would have to wait and see if anyone resigned first'. This obviously must have changed to a permanent contract at some point. Now you may all be left wondering why Rick Enning, a governor and class teacher at Meedon lower School would lie during a formal investigation. All I can think is that he was annoyed that I had rejected his sexual advances towards me, which I have now presented the school with evidence of. From October 2023 to December 2023, Rick Enning sent me multiple messages out of work hours often going well past midnight. Many of these were flirtatious and contained sexual innuendo's. It was a very difficult situation for me to navigate as he was my year lead and direct line manager. I felt I could not just ignore his messages so would respond and interact and often just laugh it off to maintain a good working relationship as I did not want him to report back to William Jenson that I was difficult to work with. I also wanted to be careful not to offend him or reject him outright. If I had fallen asleep and not continued playing online chess with him late at night, he would question me about it the next day. He would also question me about my love life or lack of it. There is a text I have presented the school, which I sent to Rick which shows this. We were discussing how I hate dating and I responded to Rick in it and I quote; 'if I'm not madly in love, it's not worth it. Never was and never will be'. End quote. THIS is the truth of who I really am as a person. THIS is the real Maria. Someone who has always believed in true love and still do. Not the woman who sent that message to William Jenson, when she was having suicidal thoughts and on the verge of a breakdown after all she endured over the year. Rick knows this. He knew I was a woman who would never sleep with a man I was not in love with, as that text message proves. William Jenson also knows this. Everyone in the school knows this. By December, I knew Rick's messages were getting too much and I spoke to a friend and she helped me change my settings so he couldn't see when I was last online. I also reduced my responses and then I think he got the message. He didn't react very well and it was awkward for about a week or two. So again, this brings me back to the question; why did Rick Enning lie in his formal statement? As well as maybe being annoyed that I had rejected his sexual advances, perhaps he was also scared that I might reveal the truth about him, so he thought he better paint me in a negative light and destroy my character first, but as we all know, the truth always reveals itself in the end. My dad often tells me a quote from the bible 'darling those who dig pits for others fall themselves into it.' Rick Enning is a married man with a child and I question his integrity as a teacher, governor, father and husband.

I would like to point out at this stage that neither Sharon Pew or Rick Enning have faced any serious consequence for their sexual misconduct in the workplace. That means employees in this school clearly get treated differently, perhaps based on the colour of their skin. It feels very unfair that out of three people who have had serious formal grievances against them in this school, the only one that has suffered immediate and harsh consequences is the one that was on the verge of a breakdown, having had suicidal thoughts from stress related to her work environment. The other two employees committed their gross misconduct in their full senses with full intent over a lengthy period of time. Mine was on one day when I was pushed to the absolute brink.

Heather Trudge has mentioned in her report that she feels there is no direct causal link or correlation between what I have endured over the year and my misconduct on the 27th June. This is a complete and utter lie, as I never would have said what I said in a million years if it wasn't for the exact sequence of events that led up to it and my mental health at the time. This is 100 percent the truth and anyone that knows me knows me knows that. So all I can take from this is that William and Rick (with the help of Heather) have decided to say whatever they need to say to dismiss me. If Sharon Pew is the role model for everyone out there and for the children of this school, then I truly worry about the next generation of children. I should have done the formal grievance against Sharon Pew a lot sooner (instead of doing what I did.) I have spent my whole life being a law abiding citizen and following all the rules in every school I have worked in, until the stress of a bad work environment completely changed my character for one day, when I was already having suicidal thoughts. The evidence of all of this is there. I have the doctors note of suicidal thoughts a week before my misconduct and Martha Dunn's statement clearly talks about what I had endured at the hands of Sharon Pew from January right the way through until July. Stacey Walliams also confirms this, but Heather Trudge has decided to completely ignore all the evidence and destroy my life instead by giving me an unjust and unfair outcome. I would like to remind you all of the film 'The boy in the striped pyjamas'. The father was happy to murder everyone else's child, but when it came to his own child, it was suddenly a different outcome. Imagine if your own child had been bullied, harassed, slandered, had racist comments made and had to endure sexual harassment in the staffroom on a daily basis and then withdrew into their classroom with migraines and headaches because of it, and then the school decided to cover up the real perpetrators crimes and punish the victim who was pushed out of character on one day and on the edge of a breakdown instead? How would you feel? I truly hope this never happens to your own child or someone you love, but if it ever does, I truly hope that whatever outcome you give me today, your own child gets exactly the same outcome. This is not me being mean. This is me actually me being completely fair and just and saying that I trust the outcome you now give me would be exactly the same outcome you would want for your own child if you found them sobbing on the bed wanting to end their own life because of all they have endured over the year. Karma is real so please don't forget that when deciding my fate.

I have always been honest throughout this process, yet Heather Trudge has tried to use my honesty against me, claiming that because I admitted and apologised for my mistake, I should be given the worst outcome possible and barred from teaching. Others have lied and I have provided the school with proof of these lies, but according to Heather Trudge lies are to be rewarded and honesty is to be condemned. Heather claims in her report I am someone who premeditates things. If I am so evil, I would not have done everything I could to help save a parent's life last year who confessed to me they had breast cancer.

I would like to end by saying that I expressed immediate remorse and regret to William for that message on the 27th June, both in my texts to him directly and in an email I sent to Nicole the next day. My actions on June 27th were not premeditated as Heather Trudge has suggested. They were a momentary lapse in judgement caused by extreme stress and a sense of injustice. My prior track record as a teacher demonstrates my commitment to professionalism and excellence. My planning was consistently thorough, and my dedication to my students and colleagues was unwavering. Witnesses such as Martha Dunn and Abraham Raft have confirmed this in their statements. Heather Trudge states that because I've been honest from the start of the investigation and owned up to this and actually shown integrity that the school should destroy my life by barring me from teaching. However, I would argue that it is not something I have ever done before or ever intend to repeat, and the mitigating factors all show it was;

1. Totally out of character - My history as a kind, compassionate, and professional individual stands in stark contrast to the portrayal in the report. My evidence shows I am a woman who believes in true love and I never talked about sex before that day on the 27th June.

2. My Mental Health - The bullying, slander, sexual harassment and unfair treatment I faced throughout the year pushed me to breaking point. I was experiencing severe work-related stress and suicidal thoughts, primarily caused by Sharon Pew and these were documented by my doctor. I have shown proof of this.

3. My previous impeccable track record – which both Abrahim Raft (the deputy headteacher) and Martha Dunn have confirmed. And

4. Immediate remorse - I apologized to William Jenson immediately after the incident in text messages and in an email to Nicole Mackintosh (the chairman of governors) on the 2nd July.

These are all mitigating factors outlined by ACAS and have not been taken into account whatsoever by Heather Trudge, Emily Herruke or the school. Even though Heather knows I was sobbing saying that I wanted to die on the day we had our meeting in July expressing my remorse for my actions on the 27th June, when she called for Abrahim Raft to support me. And she also knows that I have always told the truth, which is now being used against me in her report. Would it have been better if I had lied Heather? My parents have always taught me to be honest and I personally have huge respect for people that tell the truth no matter how hard it is. If Heather Trudge is saying that my honesty and the fact that I have always told the truth is the reason I should now be barred from teaching and have my life destroyed, then maybe I should have lied instead. But I am an honest person and this also proves that everything I have endured over the year at the hands of Sharon Pew is also true and my evidence corroborates this. It's a shame that the school decided to do a sham investigation into Sharon Pew and not investigate the sexual comments and racism properly as only then might you have realised the true extent of the problem and what I endured and empathised with how much I have truly suffered, but all the school seems to care about is covering it's own back and destroying my life instead, based on one text message I immediately apologised for. Haven't I suffered enough at Meedon or will you all not be able be happy until I'm dead? After all the injustice I have faced over the year, I am grateful to those colleagues at Meedon who have always supported me. If all my other witnesses had also been questioned about the racism and inappropriate sexual comments by Sharon Pew, I am certain that the full truth would have come out, but the school has decided to cover up the truth instead.

Finally, I am sitting here in front of you all asking you for justice and to see the truth and look beyond simply that message that I sent William Jenson on the

27th June. I was not being me on that day, but was trying to be Sharon Pew, as after having spent my whole life being 'the good girl', I realised I always lost, but women like Sharon Pew got what they wanted, i.e. the year group of their choice with 22 children. I thought that's the kind of woman that this school obviously rewards and being me (someone who all my friends and family say is actually innocent and a kind person) does not work. It's the women like Sharon Pew that always seem to win and I guess I got sick of it, especially after all I had endured at her hands over the year. It would have been very easy for me to give up and end my life after all I have endured this year. As a close friend pointed out that they will have all already have made up their mind, based on that message alone you're guilty, so what's the point? It's 7 of them against one of you and it is never going to be fair. I know you are all meant to be an impartial panel, but we all know that is simply never going to be the case. Some of you know William and Rick fairly well. They are both men in a position of authority and governors of the school. I am simply a class teacher. The only way this would ever be totally impartial and unbiased would be if it went to trial, in a court of law being judged by people who were strangers. If that is what I have to do to get justice, then of course that is what I will do.

In this school, three people have had formal grievances against them and the only person who faced any immediate consequences of suspension was someone of an ethnic background. Even though my mistake was made on the edge of a breakdown, whereas my other two other colleagues made theirs in their full senses and with intent, so why have I been made to suffer the most? After everything I have endured at Meedon, I'm not sure if I even want to teach again anyway now. So why am I here? Why am I putting myself through this when I didn't have to. It's simple. To clear my name. To speak my truth. To fight against injustice. As Johnny Depp said during his trial, whenever there is an injustice, never sit down. Always stand up and fight. He fought and he won and rightly so, as I watched his trial from start to finish. The evidence spoke for itself. If you have looked at all my evidence, you would also know this, and I have actually only presented some of it today. There is a lot more.

I strongly believe you should never try to destroy someone's life with lies, when yours can be destroyed by the truth!! I have told the truth, the whole truth and nothing but the truth since the start of this investigation. I told the truth, knowing it might get me in trouble. Not everyone in this school has told the truth as I have, because they don't want to face any consequences or admit to any wrongdoing. However, I do believe in Karma. In the words of Martin Luther King; **'an injustice anywhere is a threat to justice everywhere. We are caught in an inescapable network of mutuality, tied in a single garment of destiny. Whatever affects one directly, affects all indirectly'.** I am asking you to see the truth. And it is something I would be willing to fight for until my last dying breath. Whatever decision you make is not going to change my good character or change the truth. And the truth is everything I have said today. If you are still all going to go ahead and give me the same outcome regardless of all the evidence of my suffering at Meedon Lower School, then you are just adding to the suffering I have already endured at this school.

As well as all the evidence I have presented the school, I hope you have also had a chance to read the character references I received from four of my colleagues; Abrahim Raft, Martha Dunn, Kelvin Moche and Stacey Walliams. I would like to read just one of these now to the panel.

To whom it may concern,

I am writing to wholeheartedly support my colleague, Maria Bassett, as a dedicated and teacher and colleague. Having the pleasure of working alongside Maria since September 2023 I can confidently attest to her professional qualities that make her an asset to any educational setting.

Maria is an extremely hardworking and conscientious individual who consistently demonstrated a deep commitment to her students and her craft. Her well-organised and conscientious nature meant that she was planned ahead of time, thinking of the needs and abilities of her class. As a colleague, she strived to leave her class planned and resourced for me the following day. The only time she couldn't leave what was needed was when the other teachers hadn't planned. Her ability to think ahead and communicate effectively was , as evidenced by her emailing me the day before I covered her class to ensure a seamless transition.

Maria was always kind and supportive but the extraneous working conditions pushed her mental health to its limit. She always wanted to work as a team building strong relationships with each person she worked with. She was hesitant to draw attention to herself putting the needs of the team first taking on extra planning to support both the children and adults alike. This trait also speaks to her selflessness and dedication to the well-being of others.

Maria was open and trusting, and she shared her social anxiety with me. This made her acutely aware in social situations so she strove to always do the right thing and not cause stress or friction. She sought harmony not stress. She was never rude, crude or inappropriate in her words or actions. She was a consummate professional. It was only when her mental health became unstable after months or criticism, lude sexual comments either aimed at her or in general conversation which led to a breakdown. This breakdown affected her mentally and physically. This said it was only her strength of character and resilience that kept her going as long until the third term. She is incredibly strong in the face of adversity.

As a colleague, I have had the pleasure of witnessing Maria's teaching skills firsthand. Her passion for education, combined with her tireless work ethic and outstanding organisational skills, make her a wonderful teacher.

In conclusion, Maria Bassett is a wonderful human, who would never seek to upset anyone deliberately. Her dedication, patience, and exceptional planning skills make her a great colleague who I'd love to work with again. If you have any further questions, please do not hesitate to contact me.

Sincerely,

Martha Dunn

Chapter 31 – December 2024

Banned from driving

Nightmare! What an end to a truly nightmarish year for me. On December 2nd 2024, I had a court case and was told I was being banned from driving for 6 months due to having 12 speeding points. I had received 6 points two and a half years ago when I had lived in Huntingdon and then received 6 more while working at Meedon Lower School. The last 6 points were six months apart. I received three in January 2024 and three more in June 2024. I really should have kept an eye on my points. I argued my case in court and how difficult it would be for me to get to work and back, but it didn't make any difference. In fact, when I googled it, it would have taken me two and a half hours to get to Meedon Lower School from where I lived. I would have needed to get a train and two buses. That would have meant five hours of traveling a day, which was just not feasible. The other option was a taxi which would have cost me £50 each way, so would have been £100 per day which was £500 a week or £2000 a month. My whole salary would go on travel. I would have needed to leave Meedon Lower School in December 2024 regardless, as the commute to work and back was just not feasible for six months. I got really lucky in that I got a teaching job much closer to home. Thank you God. On my dad's advice, I bought an electric bike and could cycle to school within 20 minutes. It took 25 minutes to cycle to my gym and 30 minutes to my mums house. So far, I have only fallen off the bike once with minor scrapes and nearly hit a van in the road due to the brakes failing, but have since had the brakes tightened. I also had a trye puncture, but got it replaced for free as I'd cleverly got insurance for that. I really miss my car though now. My insurance is going to go through the roof, when I get my car back, but I have never appreciated having a car as much as I do right now. Cycling is okay when the weather is decent, but the ease of having a car and being able to throw things in the boot or get from A to B easily and quickly, has never been so missed. Please God, I pray I get my car back soon and can start driving again. Please, please, please!

Chapter 32 – September 2023

How it all began

I have just started at Meedon Lower School. It is a 2 and 3 form entry and in Year 2 there are 3 classes. I seem to have been given a very argumentative and challenging class, with one child in particular who is extremely challenging. He often throws things at the other children and then runs out of the classroom into the playground. We all have walkie talkies in each class, but mine seems to go missing all the time. I have a huge leak in the ceiling of my classroom and the caretaker Steve is often having to bring buckets into class and place them under the leaks. I then place the tables and chairs strategically to avoid this. The headteacher; William Jenson has been extremely supportive and kind to me. On training day, I took a few wrong turns driving into work and didn't actually notice that he had been driving behind me until I got to work. When we went to sit down in the hall ready for the morning training on the first day, I was sitting next to a new colleague called Alice and then suddenly heard a deep voice behind me say 'can I sit here?'

'Yeah sure', I replied, not realising until a short while later that it was actually the headteacher; Mr. Jenson. When the break came, I thought I should make a good impression, so said 'How was your summer?' 'Yeah it was really good' he replied.

'Sorry about my driving this morning, I'm just trying to get used to the route still', I commented.

'Yeah and you took a wrong turning too I noticed coming in', he responded.

'Oh yeah' I laughed, 'my sense of direction is not the best', I said, as I heard Alice giggling next to me.

'Oh God' I thought. He must have been following me for a while, as I took the wrong turn and he also was behind me for the last 15 minutes of the journey in, so I wondered why he hadn't gone the right way instead of following me.

'My daughter has just started to learn to drive', Mr. Jenson said as he started to walk over to the other side of the room to assist the new deputy headteacher, Abraham Raft with something.

Over the next few months between September and December, I noticed that Mr. Jenson seemed to favouritise me and it was the best feeling ever. One day, I was telling Charlie off in my class about the fact that he was refusing to do his work. 'Do you want to miss your breaktime doing the work Charlie?' I looked up to see Mr. Jenson smiling at me. This was such a pleasant change from my previous school, where the headteacher, Mrs. Raymond had frequently come into frown at me and tell me what I was doing wrong.

The next day Sharon Pew came into tell me that Charlie would be in her class for the day. Apparently, Mr. Jenson had said 'to give Miss. Bassett a break'. I was touched.

Another day, I asked my mum to make pakora's so I could take in to school for Diwali. I wanted people to like me. They all loved them. I left some for Mr. Jenson and Mr. Raft in their office. Later we had a staff meeting. I was sitting at the back when Mr. Jenson came in, picked up a chair from one side of the room and placed it next to me. 'Thanks for the pakora's. My children loved them. Did your mum make them? Is she married?', said Mr. Jenson as he sat down beside me and laughed, good naturedly.

'Yeah she's a really good cook', I laughed and then the meeting soon commenced.

My first few months at Meedon Lower school were amazing. I felt safe and protected and for the first time ever felt like I was finally working in a school I could stay at for a very long time, if not forever. Mr. Jenson was kind and didn't micromanage, but allowed me to just get on with my job. Rick Enning was my head of year and he was also very supportive and kind to me. In fact I noticed he would go above and beyond to help me whenever I needed it. In return I would bring him chocolates. At the start, if Sharon Pew said anything negative about me behind my back, he would tell her off and stick up for me. Sharon Pew was the other Year 2 teacher in our team and as the year progressed, I quickly learnt that I was working with someone I could not trust... someone who would end up nearly destroying my life. Sharon Pew was a liar, a gossip, someone who liked to slag people off in the staff room and spread malicious rumours, perhaps to make herself feel better about her own miserable life. She would often not do the planning properly or leave stuff until the last second. If she made a mistake and I pointed it out to her, she could not accept it and would lie to cover it up or worse blame me. On top of that, she was more than happy to criticise me at any opportunity. Working with Sharon was like working with a ticking time bomb. To begin with, I would let a lot of stuff slide, in terms of the lies and racist comments, where she said I was 'indianising things' and she 'didn't know that Indian people ate ketchup'. She was also constantly talking about sex and a lot of people at work commented on it. Rick Enning never criticised me and he was the year lead, so I'm not sure why Sharon Pew felt she needed to take it upon herself to keep coming into my classroom to tell me what to do; as if she was senior management. In July, I finally made a formal grievance against Sharon Pew, but I probably should have done it a lot sooner. If I had, I wouldn't have got angry and made my one big mistake that got me suspended. Here is my formal grievance form which lists some of the things I endured at the hands of Sharon Pew.

Nature of the grievance
Please set out the details of your complaint (e.g. what has happened, dates, times, locations, all those involved and any attempts at resolution).

Details: Gross misconduct by Sharon Pew – bullying, harassment, racism, slander, inappropriate sexual comments. Details below.

October 2023 – Year 2 Team meeting
Sharon said I 'indianise things' and I wondered what she meant by that, but I didn't feel confident enough to say anything at the time. Later I mentioned this to Abrahim as it was playing on my mind.

November 2023 – Year 2 team meeting
Sharon made sexually inappropriate remarks; bragging about oral sex, being 'naughty' at school, getting pregnant at 16 and having affairs in the workplace.

December 2023 – Year 2 Team meeting
Sharon made sexually inappropriate remarks about anal sex. She then flashed her bare bottom and said 'here touch my buns of steel'. She also emulated having sex.

December 2024 – xmas do
During end of term staff xmas do, (after I had left) Sharon revealed to me she had flashed her breasts and went to photocopy them.

January 2024
I noticed Sharon had put the wrong date on a worksheet. I let her know of her mistake and that I was happy to change it for her. She said 'No I haven't. You're confusing me'. Later she reported to Rick that 'Sorry about the wrong date. Maria confused me this morning'. I talked to Rick about it at the time.

February 2024
Before half term, Rick had distributed the planning during PPA time to me and Sharon. I was doing Maths and Maths fluency. He was doing Literacy and Shared Reading and Sharon was doing Science, PSHE and RE. On return after half term, I noticed there was no PSHE or RE planning. Sharon had copied and pasted the Autumn term planning for us, which the children had already been taught. I messaged Rick to inform him of this, but he didn't think Sharon would ever do that. He realised by end of first week back that I was right and she had done that and joked with Sharon that someone hasn't done the planning. She apologised and promised to do it. Privately she said to me 'who cares about the planning. It's just a bloody job'. Martha also mentioned to me later that she had overheard Sharon stating that RE was not an important subject to teach the children and 'who cares about Religion or

teaching it'. The following week Sharon had done the PSHE planning but not the RE. Rick approached me in the staff room and said 'Sharon said you're doing the RE'. I said 'she's never once even spoke to me about the RE'. I spoke to headteacher about this at the time and warned him that I was working with someone who kept lying and I did not trust.

March 2024 (on a Wednesday Martha Dunn was covering)

Martha informs me that William Jenson had caught her at photocopier, having left the whole class by themselves. Apparently Sharon gave her one copy of Maths worksheet at last second before she was meant to teach, as Sharon had only put planning on One Drive that morning and hadn't created worksheet until the last second. This has happened to me and Rick on a number of occasions.

April 2024

Before the Easter holidays, I offered to do the Science, RE and PSHE for the next term, as I wanted to have the planning done properly. Sharon was doing the Maths and Rick was doing the Literacy. I made power points for all the RE and PSHE lessons to help Rick with his eyes, as I know he has trouble seeing the plans and I wanted to make life as easy as possible for him. However, I noticed that all the Science units had been covered. I checked 3 times, so was sure of this. I messaged Rick and Sharon on our group whatsapp that it's all been covered. Sharon said 'no there's still stuff left'. I messaged Rick privately that there is nothing left. There is 4 units in Science which have all been covered; Plants, Materials, Animals including humans, living things and their habitats'. He said he will check with Pete who is the Science lead, but then never got back to me. After the easter half term on training day, Sharon approached me and said 'there's stuff left for Science so I'll sort it'. I replied 'really? What's left?' already knowing this was her next biggest lie. After a short pause, she then replied 'Climate change and the Environment'. I replied we've covered all the units as I checked 3 times. Climate change and environment is key stage 3 Science, not Key stage 1 Science. I told William Jenson again at the time, but he said he was not dealing with it and the Year 2 planning is Rick's domain.

May 2024 – Year 2 PPA meeting

Rick asks Sharon if she has done the Maths planning for next week and if we can see it and go through it. (Note: the previous week, Rick had informed us both that the planning all needed to be done by the previous Friday so it could be prepped ready to go for the following week. Sharon replies 'No I haven't'. Rick says 'Why haven't you done it?' Sharon says 'I don't know why. I haven't.' Rick then turned to me and said 'Maria can we go through the RE for next week?' I said yes and started to go through it. As normal Sharon started to criticise minor things about my Power point, like the LO being 'I can' instead of 'Can I.' I found this very strange considering I had actually done all the work and she had done nothing. When I finished Rick said it was brilliant. Rick then left to go and see William about something. After Rick had left the room, Sharon started to criticise Rick and make inappropriate remarks. i.e. 'Rick can fuck off. Who cares about the planning. It will get done. I'm a good teacher, that's all that matters, not the bloody planning.' I responded 'Rick is just trying to help you as we can go through and improve it like we did mine, and so we know what we're doing the following week.' She continued to criticise Rick by saying 'Rick's a bloody nob anyway, I'll do the planning when I went to. Who gives a fuck!' When Rick returned, Sharon had left. I told him she was fuming. He asked what she had said. I didn't want to hurt him, so just said 'she's just complaining about everything'.

May 2024 – In the staff room

Everyone was silent, only Sharon's booming voice could be heard. William came into eat his lunch, as Sharon was talking about escort agencies and was criticizing Simon (the cleaner).

''Simon is a right ………, but he loves you Maria, but then you encourage him. You cuddle him and stuff'.

I replied saying 'No I don't'. I felt embarrassed that she had said this in front of everyone. I didn't know how to respond at the time, but I made sure to follow this up by sending William a long email the next day (and also copied in Rick and Abrahim) and I am happy to share that with you and all the governors who know about this. I will send you the email as evidence. I also talked about this with Tracey Murrell and Carrie Barnes the following morning about how humiliated I felt when she made these comments in front of numerous witnesses.   Then I went to my classroom. Sharon came in and I explained I was busy. She continued to push for a hug. When I declined, this resulted in an argument. She went to complain to William. He responded by handing us both a code of conduct.

May 2024 – Sharon's classroom
At the end of the day, Sharon, Alice and me were in her classroom during PPA time. Sharon calls William in to see the puppets she has made. William comes in to look at them. Sharon says 'I don't have a man anymore William. I need to use my hands for something'. William responded 'Right lets get back to the puppets shall we'.   After William left, she made some inappropriate comments about William's legs.

May 2024 – Staff room
I was eating ketchup with my chips and Sharon said 'Are you actually indian?' Again I didn't challenge this as I didn't want any confrontation with an audience. William was present amongst other staff including Stacey Walliams.

June 2024
Martha called me to inform me that Sharon had made an inappropriate comment about Simon again. This was after she had been given the code of conduct by William and many more incidents have continued by Sharon after she has been handed the code of conduct by William. Sharon had said 'I wouldn't leave the kids alone with Simon'. I had left the three kids for one minute during mindful colouring club after school, just to go to the toilet and pick up something from the copier. Martha said she went to complain to William about this. Both Martha and I were perplexed as to why this would be a problem, as surely Simon would be DBS checked and William would not employ someone who was a danger to children. Again this is slandering a good man's name and character as she did mine, without any proof.

Monday 1st July, 2024

Sharon was near photocopier area and said 'I'm off my meds. I'm feeling really horny!'. This was heard by me, Chris Days and maybe Carrie.

Final Note – Throughout the year, Sharon has come into my classroom to criticise me about some minor thing, when my planning is always done and hers often is not done or is done at last second or is copied and pasted from previous term. The incidents detailed from January 2024 to the present, detail how Sharon has lied to various members of staff to belittle me and make me look bad among my colleagues. This has massively impacted my mental health over the year and made me feel really small inside. I was left feeling suicidal and had to get support from the doctor for this, who advised I take a week off. This was the reason I could not believe she was chosen to remain in Year 2, when I have worked so hard all year, often coming in super early to be prepped. In my head, I couldn't grasp how this had happened.

After handing this grievance form into the governors, an investigation was carried out. However, I found out later that this was to be a sham investigation, as only a handful of my witnesses were ever questioned. Also, the racist comments and inappropriate sexual comments were never investigated, and I discovered this directly from my witnesses. The school wanted to put all the blame on me for my one mistake, which everyone knew was totally out of character. I think the reason they didn't want to investigate properly is because they didn't want to be held liable for anything if it went to court, but I had no intention of taking this to court unless I had absolutely no other choice; all I wanted was a fair outcome for my mistake. A mistake I had apologised for immediately. However, the school still seemed determined to destroy me and have me barred from teaching. I appealed the decision and after reading my closing statement at my hearing, the decision was overturned and I got a final warning instead. It would go down as resignation on my record. Thank god, as I don't know if I would have been able to carry on living had this not been reversed, as it would have been a massive injustice. The person who should have been fired and barred from teaching was Sharon Pew. Also, Rick Enning had lied about my character and my planning in his witness statement, so he should also have had some consequences, but I'm guessing they both got away with it. How unfair and unjust life can be! After having spoken on the phone about all this to the TRA (Teaching regulation agency), they advised me to complete a form referring them both with all my evidence. In my head, the only one I wanted to potentially refer was Sharon. Yes, Rick had tried to destroy my character and reputation by lying about me and he had sent me a lot of late night inappropriate messages, but none of this would have happened if it wasn't for Sharon Pew. I kept all of the evidence on Sharon Pew and the school safe just in case one day I would ever need it in the future. However, I also wanted to move on with my life and desperately wanted peace.

Thank god for decent people in the world; Abraham Raft, Martha Dunn, Stacey Walliams, Kelvin Moche and Tracey Murrell were all a godsend as they all told the truth and supported me and each gave me amazing references.

Elouise Harrison had come to pick up my laptop on the same day I was to find out the outcome of my appeal hearing. As soon as she saw me, she started to cry and gave me a massive hug, for which I was truly grateful.

'I'm so sorry for everything you went through. I had no idea of what was going on. I've had three friends commit suicide', she stated emotionally.

'Thank you. It was all true. I should have reached out to more people and let them know how much I was suffering. Martha and Stacey and Kelvin were all aware, but I probably should have spoken up more, rather than letting it get to the point it did. I'm such an idiot. Even women that ACTUALLY are like that, don't send messages like that. I'm such an idiot', I cried.

'When do you find out? Is it today?', she asked.

'Yes, I find out today. I'm scared. Do you want to come in for a cup of tea?', I asked.

'No I have to get back to school, but take care of yourself', she said as she gave me a final hug and walked back to her car with the laptop I had given her.

Half an hour later, I got an email from Nicole Mackintosh; the chairman of governors. I had won the appeal. The final outcome on December 16th had been overturned; instead of being fired for gross misconduct, the outcome had been changed to final warning and my resignation on December 31st would now come first on my official record. This result officially meant I could have returned to my job had I not resigned. I never would make that mistake again and had it not been for Sharon Pew, I never would have made such a stupid mistake in the first place, as I was trying to be like her to prove a point; that unprofessional behaviour gets rewarded at Meedon Lower School. However, the headteacher had decided to overlook all of Sharon Pew's multiple breaches of the Meedon code of conduct and only punish my one mistake instead. A mistake I had only made to prove a point and when pushed to the absolute brink of my sanity.

I truly hope Karma exists. I withdrew my tribunal claim against the school; Bassett V's Meedon; that I would have gone ahead with had the school not changed the outcome of my case. I sent the following email to the Watford Employment Tribunal and copied in Nicole Mackintosh; the chairman of governors and Abrahim Raft; the deputy headteacher.

To whom it may concern,

As I have now received a satisfactory outcome from the school following my appeal, I now wish to withdraw my tribunal claim.

I have been told by many family and friends that I do deserve some compensation for my immense suffering at Meedon lower school and I have extensive evidence plus a doctors note BEFORE my own misconduct on 1 day, which states "stress related to my work environment and suicidal thoughts", which was directly related to the bullying, harassment, racism, slander and sexual harassment I faced by a certain employee in particular at Meedon Lower school.

However, I will now leave it to karma.
Happy Valentine's Day.

Thank you,
Maria Bassett

Strange how things turn out considering I had written the chapter below at the end of my first term at Meedon. I had genuinely believed that I had finally found a school I could stay forever and be happy in. Wishful thinking perhaps.

January 1ˢᵗ 2024

Meedon Lower School. I feel protected and safe in this school. Thank you god, for bringing these people into my life. That is enough. More than enough. I hope I am right!

I feel like I am too old for love now anyway, so I am going to relax and leave the rest to you now God. Let's see what happens!

On my death bed, let it be known, there once lived a girl, who never stopped believing in the beauty of her dreams and always followed her heart! Xxx

Printed in Great Britain
by Amazon